SPANISH SUBJUNCTIVE IN CONTEXT

Gunnar Anderson
University of Hawaii

Patricia Vilches Bustamante
University of Evansville

UNIVERSITY PRESS OF AMERICA

Lanham • New York • London

University Press of America,® Inc.
4720 Boston Way
Lanham, Maryland 20706

3 Henrietta Street
London WC2E 8LU England

Printed in the United States of America
British Cataloging in Publication Information Available

Library of Congress Cataloging-in-Publication Data

Anderson, Gunnar Jay.
Spanish subjunctive in context / Gunnar Anderson,
Patricia Vilches Bustamante.
p. cm.
1. Spanish language—Subjunctive. 2. Spanish language—
Textbooks for foreign speakers—English.
I. Bustamante, Patricia Vilches. II. Title.
PC4290.A5 1994 468.2'421—dc20 94–37957 CIP

ISBN 0–8191–9759–9 (pbk. : alk. paper)

The paper used in this publication meets the minimum requirements of American National Standard for Information Sciences—Permanence of Paper for Printed Library Materials, ANSI Z39.48–1984.

CONTENTS

Spanish Subjunctive in Context is a new type of subjunctive resource manual. The subjunctive mood is one of the most difficult foreign language concepts for English-speaking students. Spanish has a higher frequency of subjunctive than other Romance languages such as French or spoken Italian. To our knowledge there exists no student text solely devoted to the subjunctive, and this book addresses that lacuna.

The difficulty engendered by the subjunctive concept is that the context determines whether to use the indicative or the subjunctive in any given sentence. An isolated sentence can often be either indicative or subjunctive, depending on the mood of the speaker. In this way the subjunctive is vastly more difficult than learning the Spanish future tense or the Spanish present perfect tense, which closely correspond to how they function in English.

Learning the subjunctive mode can be a daunting task, since it is not immediately recognizable to all modern English speakers, nor is is frequently or regularly used by them. For the most part English speakers, at least in the United States, tend to substitute an infinitive phrase for a subjunctive one, as in "we asked him to be at the party" (infinitive), rather than "we asked that he be at the party" (subjunctive). English-speaking students will find that learning and understanding the subjunctive is essential to mastering the Spanish language itself. Students will learn, for instance, that they cannot express request, desire, demand, etc., with either the infinitive or indicative mode of a given verb, but that they are in fact obliged to use the subjunctive mode. In short, it is not easy or desirable to avoid the subjunctive in Spanish; it must be used with great frequency.

Do you think he has called? This sentence can be said in one of two ways in Spanish: *¿Crees que él ha llamado?* (indicative) or *¿Crees que él haya llamado?* (subjunctive). These sentences are not interchangeable, however, having very different connotations. The first is neutral; the speaker has no preconceived notions about the person having called or not, while the second is tinged with doubt on the questioner's part: he doesn't believe that the call has been made.

I want to speak to a secretary that knows Italian. Again there are two ways in Spanish to say this sentence. *Quiero hablar con una secretaria que habla italiano*-- this indicative sentence means that you know that there is such a secretary at the establishment; you have forgotten her name, or only spoken to her by phone without a proper introduction. *Quiero hablar con una secretaria que hable italiano*: this subjunctive sentence indicates that you don't know if such a secretary can indeed be found there.

The previous examples illustrate how the subjunctive works, but simple explanations of this type do not work well in instructing the student to "feel" the subjunctive. Students are used to viewing grammar forms as being either right or wrong in a given situation. When one deals with the subjunctive there is often no right or wrong--simply two possibilities conveying different things, but both valid sentences. Spanish Subjunctive in Context aims to provide the essential ingredient missing in traditional grammar explanations and isolated single sentence examples: the full context of the situation. By reproducing selected full-length Spanish comic strips the text recreates the environment that produced the subjunctive. By using Spanish comic strips-- Condorito, a Chilean series--only uncontrived Spanish appears, with no "artificial" expressions.

The Condorito series is written in a very good non-dialectal form of Spanish. Any unusual expressions and vocabulary that appear are fully explained in the vocabulary section facing each full-page strip. The vocabulary often repeats from strip to strip, and we feel that they provide an excellent source for day-to-day high frequency vocabulary. The strips have proven very popular in classes we have taught, and are immeasurably superior-- for the purposes of authentic subjunctive usage as well as genuine high frequency expressions--to forced and awkward Spanish translations of U.S. strips. The cultural context in Condorito is Hispanic-centered, as well.

The book begins with an introductory chapter on present tense subjunctive formation, with conjugation exercises (answers provided in a key at the end of the chapter). At this point the contextual approach begins, with present subjunctive comic strips appearing. Each comic strip occupies one page. On the facing page appears an explanation of the particular subjunctive case featured, and the reason it is used. "Anti- examples" are provided, whenever feasible, so that the student can see the non-absolute nature of the subjunctive.

The facing page also lists and defines unusual vocabulary, cultural notes, and finally provides further examples based on the discrete subjunctive point seen in the episode. At the end of each section is a translation quiz, designed to test comprehension of the type of subjunctive covered, with an answer key provided at the end of the book.

These strips are presented according to the type of subjunctive seen in the episode. The first major type is subjunctive of emotion and volition, with verbs such as *querer* (to want), *pedir* (to request), *decir* (to say), *insistir* (to insist), *esperar* (to hope) etc.

The second type examined is subjunctive triggered by the phrase *para que* (so that/ in order to), which is used more often than the corresponding phrase in English, sometimes with a special meaning, and for this reason is covered thoroughly.

The next type of subjunctive is triggered by expressions of time, such as *cuando* (when), *mientras* (while) *antes de* (before), *después de* (after) etc.

The book goes on to cover the concepts of negation, indefinite categories, present perfect subjunctive, and past subjunctive, plus a final comprehensive review of all of the uses of the subjunctive in a few specially selected episodes that contain four or five subjunctive instances each.

Forming the present subjunctive

The formation of the present subjunctive is not difficult. Let's begin with a brief overview of the subjunctive, starting with the "ar" class of verbs. (N.B. : the vosotros form is not dealt with in this book as it is not used in Latin America)

Indicative		Subjunctive	
hablo	hablamos	hable	hablemos
hablas		hables	
habla	hablan	hable	hablen

The subjunctive treats the "ar" verbs more or less as if they were "er".
Fill in the blanks with the subjunctive form.

A. 1. yo bailo = que yo ______________
2. ellos necesitan = que ellos ______________
3. tú preparas = que tú ______________
4. Ud. canta = que Ud. ______________

Let's look at the verb "comprender" to introduce the “er” type. We will use the "ar" endings here.

Indicative		Subjunctive	
comprendo	comprendemos	comprenda	comprendamos
comprendes		comprendas	
comprende	comprenden	comprenda	comprendan

B. 1. yo leo = que yo ______________
2. ellos venden = que ellos ______________
3. tú crees = que tú ______________
4. nosotros comemos = que nosotros ______________

The last category is the “ir” verbs. These will also take the "ar" endings

Indicative		Subjunctive	
vivo	vivimos	viva	vivamos
vives		vivas	
vive	viven	viva	vivan

C. 1. yo abro = que yo ______________
2. tú recibes = que tú ______________
3. ellos deciden = que ellos ______________
4. Ud. escribe = que Ud. ______________

Many verbs are slightly irregular in the subjunctive. Most verbs are not as simple as those that we just looked at.

1. "Ar" verbs will sometimes need a spelling change to preserve their original sound.
The verb "sacar" will be conjugated as follows:

saque	saquemos
saques	
saque	saquen

The verb "llegar" (also "entregar" etc.) will also need a spelling change to preserve the verb's sound:

llegue	lleguemos
llegues	
llegue	lleguen

2. Verbs with an irregular "yo" form in the present, such as:
decir (digo), poner (pongo), salir (salgo), hacer (hago), traer (traigo), tener (tengo), venir (vengo), valer (valga), etc. all keep the irregular stem throughout the subjunctive.

Indicative		Subjunctive	
digo	decimos	diga	digamos
dices		digas	
dice	dicen	diga	digan

3. The "ar" and "er" stem changing verbs, like entender (Ud. entiende), poder (Ud. puede), cerrar (Ud. cierra), follow the same pattern in the subjunctive.

Indicative		Subjunctive	
quiero	queremos	quiera	queramos
quieres		quieras	
quiere	quieren	quiera	quieran

4. The "ir" stem changing verbs, e.g. mentir (Ud. miente), sentir (Ud. siente), morir (Ud. muere), function as above, but will have an irregular change in the "nosotros" form.

Indicative		Subjunctive	
duermo	dormimos	duerma	durmamos
duermes		duermas	
duerme	duermen	duerma	duerman

"Ir" verbs like "servir" and "pedir" (e>i) will keep their irregularity throughout:

sirva	sirvamos	pida	pidamos
sirvas		pidas	
sirva	sirvan	pida	pidan

5. Finally, there are a few irregulars that don't fit any pattern.
ir = vaya, vayas, etc.
estar = esté, estés, etc.
ser = sea, seas, etc.
dar = dé, des, etc.
ver = vea, veas, etc.
haber = haya, hayas, etc.
saber = sepa, sepas, etc.

D.

1. yo busco =	que yo	____________
2. ellos se destacan =	que ellos se	____________
3. María busca =	que María	____________
4. ellos ponen =	que ellos	____________
5. nosotros vamos =	que nosotros	____________
6. ellos son =	que ellos	____________
7. él siente =	que él	____________
8. ellos encuentran =	que ellos	____________
9. ella conoce =	que ella	____________
10. yo conduzco =	que yo	____________
11. tú explicas =	que tú	____________
12. Juan sale =	que Juan	____________

Forming the past (imperfect) subjunctive

Let's look at a simple "ar" verb to begin. The "ar" endings are

ara	áramos
aras	
ara	aran

An example is "cantar"

cantara	cantáramos
cantaras	
cantara	cantaran

Do not confuse this with the future tense. If you pronounce it aloud, you will see that it is quite different!

"Er" and "ir" verbs take these endings:

iera	iéramos
ieras	
iera	ieran

For example:	escribiera	escribiéramos
	escribieras	
	escribiera	escribieran

The irregular verbs in the past subjunctive follow the irregulars stems from the preterite tense. As you will recall, in the preterite "querer" goes to "quise, quisiste" etc. "Poder" goes to "pude, pudiste" etc. These irregular stems give us the stem for the past subjunctive:

quisiera	quisiéramos
quisieras	
quisiera	quisieran

All you need to do is recall the list of irregular preterite verbs. Here goes!

saber = supe, supiste, etc.	= so past subjunctive is supiera, supieras, etc.
hacer = hice, hiciste, etc.	= so past subjunctive is hiciera, hicieras, etc.
decir = dije, dijiste	= so dijera, dijeras (the "i" drops from the ending here, as in "trajera")
traer= traje, trajiste	= trajera, trajeras
ir = fui, fuiste	= fuera, fueras (the "i" drops here)
tener = tuve, tuviste	= tuviera, tuvieras
poner = puse, pusiste	= pusiera, pusieras
ser = fui, fuiste	= fuera, fueras

The " ir" stem changing verbs are also a little different here, just as they are in the present subjunctive. In the past subjunctive simply follow the third person plural (Uds., ellos or ellas) stem from the preterite: sentir= sintieron, pedir= pidieron, advertir= advirtieron, etc. These keep the specific irregularity throughout the whole conjugation:
dormir = durmiera, durmieras, etc.
sentir = sintiera, sintieras, etc.
pedir = pidiera, pidieras, etc.
advertir = advirtiera, advirtieras, etc.
pedir = pidiera, pidieras, etc.

E. Put these forms in the past subjunctive:
1. yo/ querer
2. ellos/ insistir
3. ella/ pedir
4. tú/ decir
5. nosotros/ ir
6. ella/ hablar
7. nosotros/ bailar
8. yo/ tener
9. Uds. / ser
10. él/ saber
11. Ud./ decir
12. yo/ servir

Subjunctive formation

Answers

A.
1. baile
2. necesiten
3. prepares
4. cante

B.
1. lea
2. vendan
3. creas
4. comamos

C.
1. abra
2. recibas
3. decidan
4. escriban

D.
1. busque
2. destaquen
3. busque
4. pongan
5. vayamos
6. sean
7. sienta
8. encuentren
9. conozca
10. conduzca
11. expliques
12. salga

E.
1. quisiera
2. insistieran
3. pidieran
4. dijeran
5. fuéramos
6. hablara
7. bailáramos
8. tuviera
9. fueran
10. supiera
11. dijera
12. sirviera

Section I

Emotion/ Volition

POETA
A MÍ ME ENCANTA QUE SEAS UN POETA, CONDORITO... Y NO SOLO A MÍ.
¿Y A QUIÉN MÁS LE AGRADA?
26.278
A MI PAPÁ.
¿EN SERIO?
SÍ, PORQUE MI NOVIO ANTERIOR EL QUE CORRIÓ... ¡ERA BOXEADOR!
¡PLOP!

RECUERDO
¡HIP!
¿DÓNDE ESTABAS, TRUHÁN?
22.401
ESTE... ¡HIP! NO RECUERDO.
¡TENDRÁS QUE RECORDAR O TE PESARÁ!
¡ES MEJOR QUE NO ME LO HAGAS RECORDAR, PORQUE REGRESO DE INMEDIATO! ¡HIP!
¡PLOP!

Poeta

un poeta: a poet. Like dentista, guitarrista, etc., the gender of this word is determined by the article: un poeta, una poeta; the ending of poeta doesn't change.

agradar: to like; functions like gustar or interesar: me agrada, te agrada, etc.

anterior: former.

corrió: he chased away (lit. he ran). → correr a algn → to chuck somebody out

Subjunctive

#1 me encanta que <u>seas</u> : I'm delighted that you <u>are</u> a poet. Yayita's emotion tinges the "you are" and makes it become <u>seas</u> rather than "eres". Basic verbs of emotion such as gustar, desear, querer, encantar, all take subjunctive when two people are involved. First comes the verb of emotion, next the word "que" and finally the second verb- in the subjunctive. *I want George to study*. This sentence has the emotional trigger "want". It also has two people and two verbs. We must supply the word "that", however, as if the sentence were " I want that George study" = *Quiero que George <u>estudie</u>.*
She wants me to buy the book. We need this sentence to fit into the triple structure just outlined: verbal trigger, "que" and subjunctive verb:

Ella quiere / que / yo <u>estudie</u>. compre el libro

Notice that the word "me" disappeared. In Spanish this word would be "me", yet it doesn't appear in the sentence. This is because in Spanish the sentence reads "She wants that I buy the book".
Finally, verbs like gustar, querer, encantar <u>do not always take the subjunctive</u>. We need a change of subject for the subjunctive to occur.
I want to study = Quiero estudiar , because there is only one person involved. However, *She wants her brother to study* will take the subjunctive: *Ella quiere que su hermano <u>estudie</u>.*

Recuerdo

truhán: bum, vagabond, rogue

te pesará: it will cost you. → you'll be sorry, you'll regret it

de inmediato: immediately

Subjunctive

#3 Es mejor que no me lo hagas recordar: It's best that you don't make me remember (remind me). "Es mejor" can be classified as an emotional trigger for the subjunctive. *It's best that she arrive before the exam = Es mejor que <u>llegue</u> antes del examen.*

EXAMEN
ADIÓS, MAMÁ.
¿PARA DÓNDE VAS TAN APRISA, HIJITA?
¿ACASO NO TE ACUERDAS QUE HOY TENÍA CONSULTA CON EL MÉDICO?
AH, SÍ, LO HABÍA OLVIDADO.
ACUÉRDATE DE LO QUE TE DIJE. NO PERMITAS QUE EL MÉDICO TE EXAMINE SIN ROPA.
DESPREOCÚPATE, MAMÁ...
...LE EXIGIRÉ QUE ESTÉ COMPLETAMENTE VESTIDO.
¡PLOP!

SINCERIDAD
¡DISCULPEN!
¡SALUD, GARGANTA!
¡SALUD, CONDORITO!
GARGANTA. LLAMÓ TU ESPOSA PARA AVISARTE QUE MURIÓ TU TU SUEGRA.
DILE QUE COMIENCE A LLORAR. ¡YA VOY PARA ALLÁ!
¡PLOP!
¡PLOP!

Examen

tan aprisa: in such a hurry. Also "con tanta prisa".

hijita: daughter. Spoken Spanish often uses the diminutive form: "right now" is "ahorita", "grandmother" becomes " abuelita", etc.

acaso: possibly (untranslatable). Often used in questions, "acaso" has a slight sarcastic connotation- e.g. " ¿Acaso no lo estoy haciendo ahora?"= " Aren't I doing that right now?"

despreocúpate: relax (lit. unworry yourself).

Subjunctive

#1 no permitas que el médico te examine: Don't permit the doctor to examine you. Permitir, mandar, exigir, dejar, pedir are all verbs of volition or will. They can take the subjunctive when there are two people and two verbs in a sentence. Don't be fooled by the English translation "Don't permit the doctor to examine you". Even though this uses the infinitive in English, in Spanish we need the subjunctive. We must think of the sentence as being " Don't permit that the doctor examine you". *Marta asks me to go = Marta me pide que vaya.*

#4 Le exigiré que esté vestido: I will demand that he be dressed. This is the same volition-type of subjunctive as the previous one. *I insist that they leave = Insisto en que ellos se vayan. They don't permit us to smoke = No permiten que fumemos.*

Sinceridad

disculpen: excuse me. The verb "disculpar" is often used instead of "perdón."

salud: cheers! (lit. health).

suegra: mother-in-law (father-in-law is "suegro").

dile: tell her. This the tú command " di" + le. The tú commands connected to pronouns are sometimes momentarily unrecognizable to students. "Tenme la puerta" (Hold me the door), "Hazlo ahora" (Do it now), "Ponlo en la mesa" (Put it on the table). Be on the lookout for these!

ya: already. I'm already on my way. The word "ya" is used much more than its English counterpart. " Estamos ya listos" (We're ready-- not We're already ready).

Subjunctive

#3 dile que comience a llorar: tell her to start crying. "Decir" will trigger the subjunctive when it is an indirect command. *I tell him to open the door = Le digo que abra la puerta.* "Decir" will not take the subjunctive when it is stating a fact or observation: *I tell her that the book is long = Le digo que el libro es largo. He tells me it's raining = Me dice que llueve.*

ACTOR frustrado
¡ESTO DE TRABAJAR EN EL TEATRO LE DA A UNO CIERTA IMPORTANCIA!
LARI LARA
¡OYE, CONDORITO! ¿SERÍAS CAPAZ DE REPRESENTAR UN PAPEL EN LA FUNCIÓN DE ESTA NOCHE? ¡SÓLO TIENES QUE APRENDERTE UNA FRASE!
¡SÍ, SEÑOR!
¡SEÑOR MARQUÉS, UNA CARTA PARA USTED!... ¡SEÑOR MARQUÉS, UNA CARTA PARA USTED!... ¡SEÑOR MARQUÉS, UNA CARTA PARA USTED!...
A LA HORA DE LA FUNCIÓN...
¡ESPERA, YO TE AVISARÉ EL MOMENTO PRECISO EN QUE DEBES ENTRAR A ESCENA!
¡QUÉ BIEN ME QUEDÓ LA LIBREA!
UN RATO DESPUÉS...
¿PUEDO ENTRAR YA, JEFE?
¡NO, NO, FALTA TODAVÍA, ESTAMOS EN EL PRIMER ACTO!
SEGUNDO ACTO...
¿ME TOCA AHORA?
¡NO! ¡TODAVÍA NO!... ¡PACIENCIA!... ¡ESPERA!
TERCER ACTO...
¿ENTRO AHORA, JEFE? ¡ESTOY NERVIOSO!
¡ME VAS A VOLVER LOCO! ¡YO TE AVISARÉ! ¿ENTIENDES?
¡AHORA! ¡ENTRA!
¡AL FIN!... ¡MI OPORTUNIDAD!
¡SEÑOR MARQUÉS, UNA CARTA PARA USTED!
¡OOOH! ¡DEMASIADO TARDE!
¡REFLAUTA!... ¿VE USTED?... ¡HACE MÁS DE UNA HORA QUE LE ESTOY DICIENDO AL ESTÚPIDO DEL DIRE, QUE ME DEJE ENTREGARLE ESTA CARTA!...
¡PLOP!

el/la dire (=el/la director(a))

Actor

cierta importancia: a certain importance. Putting the word "cierta" in front of the noun changes its meaning. "Información cierta" means "correct information", while "cierta información" means "a certain (piece) of information".

representar un papel: to play a role (as an actor). "Desempeñar un papel" also means to play a role, not necessarily as an actor: e.g:
Oil plays a role in international politics = El petroleo desempeña un papel en la política internacional.

función: show

la librea: the livery; a servant's outfit, uniform

¿Puedo entrar ya?: Can I enter now? The use of "ya" has already been seen.

¿me toca ahora? : Is it my turn?
It's Mike's turn to decide = Le toca a Mike decidir.

entregar: to deliver

Subjunctive

#11 Hace más de una hora que le estoy diciendo al dire que me deje entregarle la carta: I've been telling the director for an hour to let me deliver the letter. Again we see "decir" triggering the subjunctive. *I've told him a thousand times to work harder = Le he dicho mil veces que trabaje más.*
She says for us to study carefully =Ella nos dice que estudiemos con cuidado.
Again, caution; if the sentence is an observation rather than a command, there is no subjunctive. *I tell them that the University has many students = Les digo que la universidad tiene muchos alumnos.*
She tells me that he is not at home = Ella me dice que él no está en casa.

frustrar → frustrate, thwart
frustrarse → to be frustrated, to miscarry or fail (plans, etc)

quedar a algn → to fit, suit (se dice de ropa)

A LA SEGURA
¿PERO, COMPADRE, NO ME DIJO QUE HABÍA SACADO CARNET PARA MANEJAR?
ASÍ ES, CUMPA.
¿ENTONCES, CÓMO ES QUE ANDA A PIE Y NO EN AUTO?
FIGÚRESE, CUMPA, CON LO QUE ME COSTÓ CONSEGUIR EL CARNET, VOY A ANDAR POR AHÍ ARRIESGÁNDOME A QUE ME LO QUITEN... ¡AH, NO!
¡PLOP!

ÓPERA
¡ACUÉRDATE QUE ESTA NOCHE TENEMOS QUE SALIR!...
¿ADÓNDE?
EL HOCICÓN
¡PERO, CUASI!... ESTA NOCHE DEBUTA MI PRIMA EN LA ÓPERA.
¡VERDAD!...
Y ENCUENTRO QUE LA MÁS ELEMENTAL DELICADEZA EXIGE QUE LE ENVIEMOS FLORES.
¡Y LA MÁS ELEMENTAL SINCERIDAD, QUE LE TIREMOS TOMATES!
¡PLOP!

A la segura

había sacado carnet para manejar: that you had gotten a driver's license. "Sacar" is the verb used for applying for or receiving documents (and grades). "Carnet" can mean any type of I.D. card.

cumpa: buddy. This word is short for "compadre" or son of one's godfather. Condorito always uses the "usted" form with Cumpa, which may seem a bit strange. This is not an uncommon usage in that "Usted" marks the relationship as a special one. For instance, in Chilean usage, the "Usted" form might be used between boyfriend and girlfriend.

figúrese: think about it.

Subjunctive

#3 voy a andar por ahí arriesgándome a que me lo <u>quiten</u> : I'm going to go around risking that they take it from me? The trigger verb is arriesgar--to risk. "I risk that they take" takes mandatory subjunctive, because "to risk" is an emotion type verb. We have two actors in the sentence, and we have the word "que". This verb <u>will not</u> take subjunctive if there is only one person in the sentence: e.g. *I risk tripping with these heavy books = Arriesgo tropezarme con estos libros pesados.*

Opera

debuta: she debuts

delicadeza: refined sentiments

<u>El Hocicón</u> : The big snout. This is the humorous name of Condorito's small-town newspaper, and will be seen again. "Hocico" means an animal snout. The "ón" suffix means "big" or " exaggerated." "Librón" means a big book or volume. "Señorón" means a bossy guy who acts like a big-shot.

Subjunctive

#3 exige que le <u>enviemos</u>: (it) demands that we send flowers.
I demand that he return the book to me =Exijo que me devuelva el libro. The teacher demands that we study more = El profesor nos exige que estudiemos más. But *The teachers demand more money* has no subjunctive, because there is only one verb, and only one agent. *The teachers demand that we pay them more* will, however, take subjunctive. *Los profesores exigen que les paguemos más.*

#4 (exige que) le <u>tiremos</u> tomates: (demands that) we throw tomatoes. The trigger " exige que" is actually in the previous frame of the cartoon, like the following example.
(Johnny) "*I hope that Santa brings us a guitar*" -- (Mikey) "*and brings us some some strings, too.*"
(Johnny) "*Ojalá que San Nicolás nos <u>traiga</u> una guitarra*"-- (Mikey) "*y que nos <u>traiga</u> también unas cuerdas.*"

el estante → shelf (in a shop)

Quiz I: Emotion / Volition

Translate the following items. Suggested answers are at the back of the text.

1. I'm delighted (encantar) that you (tú) understand mechanics.

2. They want us to buy them the notebook.

3. It's best that you (Uds.) go to the airport early.

4. The boss doesn't let us smoke in the office.

5. I demand that they pay more attention to details.

6. The dentists tells me to make an appointment for next month.

7. If you wait too long you risk the book not being on the shelf.

8. It's a good thing that you (Ud.) know so many languages.

9. I propose that we meet again next week.

10. It's to be hoped for that he doesn't forget the assignment.

11. I ask you (tú) to help me with the project.

12. I don't want them to arrive early.

13. I am delighted that you come to my house so often.

14. It really bothers my teacher that I answer in English during class.

15. Mom is always asking us to make our beds.

hacer la cama = make a/the bed

Section II

Para que

AFEITADA
¡HAY ALGO QUE ME TIENE INTRIGADO, UNGENIO!
¿SÍ?... ¿QUÉ ES?
16.553
¿PARA QUÉ USAS TRES MÁQUINAS DE AFEITAR AL MISMO TIEMPO?
¡PARA QUE LA AFEITADA ME DURE TRES DÍAS!
¡PLOP!

¡IMITAR
...Y AHORA SE VA A COMER TODA LA COMIDA Y SE VA A LA CAMA PARA QUE MAÑANA VAYA A LA ESCUELA MUY TEMPRANO Y...
¡YUYITO, DEJA LA MUÑECA Y NO LE HABLES IMITANDO A LA NIÑERA! ¡NO QUIERO QUE LA IMITES MÁS!
15 900
...Y AHORA VE A DARLE UN BESO A TU TÍO CONDORITO, QUE ACABA DE LLEGAR.
¿EN QUÉ QUEDAMOS, TÍA?
...¿NO DICES QUE NO DEBO IMITAR A LA NIÑERA?
PLOP!

Afeitada

intrigado: intrigued.

máquinas de afeitar: razors. "Afeitar(se)" means to shave.

al mismo tiempo: at the same time. "A la vez" is also a common way to say this. "El puede tocar la guitarra y cantar a la vez".

Subjunctive

#3 para que la afeitada me dure tres días: so that the shave lasts me three days. Ungenio uses subjunctive here because there are two separate verbs connected by a "para que", even though the first verb clause is only understood. " (I use three razors) so that the shave lasts me three days." "Para que" always requires subjunctive!
I open the door so that the dog (can) come in. = Abro la puerta para que entre el perro. However, *I study in order to get good grades* will not take subjunctive. Why not? Because there is only one person, only one conjugated verb. *Estudio para sacar buenas notas*. There is no "para que" in that sentence.
I beat eggs in order to make the omelette similarly has no subjunctive, while *I beat the eggs so that my mother can finish the omelette* will take subjunctive. *Yo bato los huevos para que mi mamá pueda terminar la tortilla.*

Imitar

Yuyito: Yayita's niece.

niñera: babysitter.

ve: go! This is the irregular tú command.

acaba de llegar: he just arrived. "Ellos acaban de comer" =" They just ate" (or they have just eaten).

¿En qué quedamos?: Where do we stand? (on this issue).

Subjunctive

#1 se va a la cama para que mañana vaya a la escuela: go to bed so that tomorrow you go to school.

#2 no quiero que imites a la niñera: I don't want you to imitate the baby sitter. This is the emotion/ volition type of subjunctive already seen. *He wants me to finish the book = El quiere que yo termine el libro.*
I don't want the teacher to see me = No quiero que la profesora me vea.

= por ser ladrones

el robo = theft

el cuartel = barracks

Robo

reflauta: shucks, heck. This expression isn't really used, and corresponds to Charlie Brown's expression "Good grief" which is seldom used in spoken English.

atajar = vt ① stop, intercept, cut off vi. ② take a short cut

atrasado: late.

atájenlo: cut him off.

el alcance: catch (lit: reach) from "alcanzar".

cabo: corporal. Military and police rank require "mi" in direct address: e.g. mi general, mi sargento.

la comisaría = police station, precinct

denuncia: complaint, statement.

despojo: theft. This is a rather bureaucratic term. = plundering

agarrar: to seize, to capture.

Subjunctive

#7 pasemos al archivo para que vea si puede reconocer al ladrón: Let's go to the archive in order for you to see if you can recognize the thief. This is a typical straightforward "para que" sentence. *I'm going to buy the magazine so that you (can) see the article = Voy a comprar la revista para que veas el artículo.*

She needs to go to the library so that the librarian (can) make her a bibliography = Ella necesita ir a la biblioteca para que la bibliotecaria le haga una bibliografía.

Remember if there's only one person or conjugated verb, there will be no subjunctive.

He studies hard in order to pass his classes = El estudia mucho para aprobar sus clases.

Also *I study hard in order to please my parents* . Here we see other people--parents-- but there is no verb for them. There can be no subjunctive. *Yo estudio* mucho *para complacer a mis padres.*

urgir = to be urgent pressing

urgir a algn + inf = to have to + inf

alcanzar a hacer algo = lograr hacer algo

AMANDA
¡MUCHACHOS, SE ACABÓ LA ALEGRÍA! VIENE EL INFELIZ DEL COSTAL DE PLOMO.
¡Y SE VE MUY CONTENTO!
¡HOLA A TODOS, MENOS A UNO!
¡YA EMPEZASTE, TARADO!
¡UN MOMENTO! ¡NADA DE PLEITOS NI DISCUSIONES!
23,512
¡YA SON BASTANTE GRANDECITOS PARA QUE ANDEN CON TONTERÍAS!
TIENES RAZÓN, HUEVITO, YO CON PEPE NO DEBEMOS PELEAR. ¿NO ES CIERTO?
SÍ, CONDORITO.
OYE, PEPE, ¿POR QUÉ VIENES TAN CONTENTO?
ES QUE CONOCÍ A LA LINDA Y DULCE AMANDA, Y CUANDO LE PROPUSE MATRIMONIO...
...ELLA DEJÓ CAER SU DELICADA CABECITA SOBRE MI HOMBRO Y LLORÓ COPIOSAMENTE... LUEGO ECHÓ SUS HERMOSOS BRAZOS SOBRE MI CUELLO Y...
¡NO SIGAS, COSTAL DE PLOMO, NO SIGAS!
¿Y POR QUÉ?
¡PORQUE TODO LO QUE VIENE YA LO SÉ...!
...¡AMANDA Y YO LO ENSAYAMOS VARIAS VECES!
¡PLOP!

Amanda

costal de plomo: sack of lead. Here we are introduced to Condorito's enemy, Pepe Cortisona. In Spanish "pesado" means boring and annoying, as does anything conveying the idea of weight. "Una broma pesada" means a boring or annoying joke.

infeliz: wretched.

tarado: stupid. (2) idiot — (1) impaired, physically imperfect, defective

pleito: argument, dispute. In Spanish the word "argumento" means a plotline: e.g. "La vida es sueño de Calderón tiene un argumento bastante complicado".
→ lawsuit, litigation, legal action

tonterías: foolishness.

copiosamente: copiously, excessively.

ensayar: to practice, test, try out, rehearse

Subjunctive

#3 Ya son bastante grandecitos para que anden con tonterías: You are really old to be going around so foolishly. This "para que" is different than what we've seen, and the effect is rather more subtle. It doesn't convey the idea of purpose-- in order to--but rather a comparison between what they are-- adults-- and their juvenile behaviour.

¡SOCORROOO...!
CIELOS, ESA ES LA VOZ DEL LOCO CONDORITO...
26.635
¿QUÉ LE HABRÁ PASADO AHORA? ESPERO QUE NO SEA NADA GRAVE...
¿QUÉ TE PASA, CONDORITO?
DOCTOR, AYÚDEME, POR FAVOR.
¡ESTÁ BIEN! PERO DIME, ¿QUÉ TE PASA?
DOCTOR, SOÑÉ QUE ME COMÍA UNA VACA, DESPUÉS ME COMÍA UN CERDO...
...DESPUÉS ME COMÍ UN CABRITO...
...LUEGO ME COMÍ UN ANTÍLOPE...
PERO ESO NO ES PARA QUE PIDAS SOCORRO, PUES CONDORITO.
¡CÓMO QUE NO, BABOSO, TARADO! NO ME PUEDO LEVANTAR...
¡PLOP!
...PORQUE ESTOY TAPADO CON LOS HUESOS DE LOS ANIMALES QUE ME COMÍ.

Socorro

cielos: heavens.

qué le habrá pasado: what could have happened to him. The simple future and future perfect are often used to indicate probability. " El tendrá mucha plata" = "He probably has a lot of money".

cerdo: pig.

cabrito: kid, young goat.

baboso: drooling (idiot).

tapado: covered (from tapar).

Subjunctive

#7 pero eso no es para que pidas socorro: but that's not (anything) that you should call for help (about). This "para que" is also unusual. Like the previous one, it is more in the nature of a comparison than "for the purpose of." Compared to something serious this isn't a case for one to yell for help about. *Lo del examen no es para que te vuelvas loca = This examen business isn't something to get crazy about.*

Quiz II: Para que

1. It's too early for us to go to the party.

____

2. I work hard so that the boss appreciates me.

____

3. They left a list on the table for me to do the shopping

____

4. For there to be peace in the world we need more understanding.

____

5. So that you don't get confused you can find the answers in the last pages.

____

6. I' m going to help my brother so that he can leave early.

____

7. She's going to hand the composition in today so that the teacher returns it to her sooner.

____

8. The cat meows a lot so that her owner wakes up in the morning.

____

Section III

Dudar/ Creer/ Parecer

CONDORITO
¡TODO EL DÍA JUEGA CON LA PELOTA DE GOMA!...
S.C.-623
SEMANAS, MESES LLEVA ASÍ. ALGO LE ESTÁ FALLANDO AL VIEJO. LO MEJOR SERÍA CONSULTAR A UN PSIQUIATRA.
DR. JUAN CACUMEN PSIQUIATRA
BUENAS TARDES, DOCTOR.
¡ADELANTE!
RECUÉSTESE AHÍ Y PÓNGASE CÓMODO.
NO VENGO POR MÍ, DOCTOR. VENGO POR MI ABUELITO.
ENTONCES, TOME ASIENTO Y DÍGAME QUÉ TIENE SU ABUELITO...
¡CREO QUE ESTÁ LOCO! IMAGÍNESE, DOCTOR, QUE SE PASA EL DÍA ENTERO JUGANDO CON UNA PELOTITA DE GOMA Y NO LA SUELTA MÁS.
BUENO, BUENO... NO CREO QUE SEA PARA TANTO.
PROBABLEMENTE HAYA EN ÉL SÍNTOMAS DE SENILIDAD, PERO NO LE HACE DAÑO A NADIE.
¿CÓMO QUE NO? DESPUÉS DE TODO... ¡LA PELOTA ES MÍA!
¡PLOP!

Pelota

goma: rubber.

lleva así: he's been going on like that. " Llevo 3 meses estudiando chino"=" I've been studying Chinese for 3 months." This can also be expressed by "Hace 3 meses que estudio chino". Spanish always uses these present tense constructions, while English requires the present perfect to convey the same meaning.

recuéstese= acuéstese.

no la suelta: he doesn't release it (soltar). → let go of, release, drop

hacer daño: to harm, to hurt (s.o.). My foot hurts : Me duele el pie. However, "the little boy hurts the dog when he plays like that" = "El chiquito le hace daño al perro cuando juega así."

Subjunctive

#9 no creo que sea para tanto: I don't believe it's such a big deal. Not believing requires subjunctive, while believing is generally indicative. *I believe she is in the office = Creo que ella está en la oficina.*
They don't believe that she knows him = No creen que ella lo conozca.
I don't believe that they have much time = No creo que tengan mucho tiempo.
A question that expresses doubt on the part of the questioner will take subjunctive.
Do you think María is coming to the party? (The speaker doubts it) = *¿Crees que venga a la fiesta María?*

#10. probablemente haya : there probably are. "Probablemente" doesn't require the subjunctive, but can take it. If you use the subjunctive you are injecting extra doubt into the sentence. "Es probable que", however, always takes subjunctive. *Es probable que ellos no lo entiendan.*

ponerse cómodo/a = get comfortable, make oneself comfortable

ser para tanto = to be so bad as all that, to be such a big deal

CONDORITO
UN VOLUNTARIO PARA UNA MISIÓN PELIGROSA... ¡UN PASO AL FRENTE!
¡NO EMPUJEN, DESGRACIADOS!
¡A SU ÓRDEN MI CAPITÁN!
¡BRAVO! VEO QUE EN MI SECCIÓN NUNCA FALTA UN VALIENTE Y ESTA VEZ ES EL SOLDADO CONDORITO.
NECESITO UN RECONOCIMIENTO TOTAL DEL TERRENO Y LA POSICIÓN DE LAS FUERZAS ENEMIGAS PARA SABER SI PODEMOS AVANZAR...
¡A SU ÓRDEN MI CAPITÁN!
TU MISIÓN ES DECISIVA, PERO SUMAMENTE PELIGROSA. SI TE DESCUBREN, DATE POR MUERTO... ¡BUENA SUERTE!
NO SE VE AL ENEMIGO POR NINGUNA PARTE... LLEGARÉ HASTA ESAS CASAS Y REGRESARÉ...
UNAS HORAS DESPUÉS...
¡COMO TARDA ESE HOMBRE! SEGURAMENTE LO HAN DESCUBIERTO...
¡NO! YA REGRESA... ¡Y VIENE CORRIENDO!
¡MI CAPITÁN, EL CAMPO ESTÁ LIBRE! PUEDEN PASAR CAMIONES, JEEPS Y TANQUES!...
...PERO DUDO QUE PODAMOS PASAR NOSOTROS LOS DE INFANTERÍA...
¿POR QUÉ HOMBRE?
¡PORQUE EN ESAS CASAS HAY UNOS PERROS MUY BRAVOS, QUE MUERDEN MUY FUERTE!
¡PLOP!

Voluntario adj. voluntary
n. volunteer (mil, +)

empujar: to push.

desgraciados: wretches.

sumamente: extremely.

date por muerto: (one of the tú commands with an appended pronoun) play dead.

muerden: they bite (morder).

Subjunctive

#10 dudo que podamos pasar: I doubt we can pass. The verb dudar will take subjunctive in the positive, and indicative in the negative. (Latin American Spanish, however, tends to retain the subjunctive even in the negative structure of dudar: No dudo que sea así) *We don't doubt that she has the book. = No dudamos que ella tiene el libro*. Again, as in the previous sections, for subjunctive to occur we need two people and two different conjugated verbs.
I doubt I can pass the exam will not be subjunctive: *Dudo poder aprobar el examen.*
However, *She doubts that I need her help = Ella duda que yo necesite su ayuda.*
The teacher doesn't believe that I know the material = El profesor no cree que yo sepa la materia.

darse por muerto = to play dead

dar por muerto a algn = to give someone up for dead.

llegar a hacer algo = to reach the point of doing something

gracias anticipadas = thanks in advance

echar humo = to smoke

Carta

callo: callus , corn

¡Qué carta más curiosa!: what a strange letter! The noun and adjective can be changed within this idiomatic structure: e.g. " ¡Qué hombre más loco!" = "What a crazy man!"; "What a long book!" would be "¡Qué ______ más _______!"

Me parte el corazón: it breaks my heart. This is a fixed expression, sometimes expressed with the reflexive: "Se me parte el corazón." partir, arrancar, romper

Se los enviaré: I will send them to him. The "se" here replaces " le" when used in conjunction with a direct object pronoun like " lo". " I will read it (la revista) to her" = "Se la leeré."

ñato: guy. This is a term from South America, and is used especially in Chile. In Mexico the term "cuate" is used; in Spain "tío", and so forth. The best general Spanish word is probably "tipo", as it is understood everywhere.

Subjunctive

#5 te ruego me ayudes: I beg you to help me. This is the emotion-volition class of subjunctive. The "que" is left out here (Te ruego que me ayudes.) This is acceptable in certain cases, in both written and spoken Spanish, but is not recommended for the neophyte. The omission conveys a certain elegance to the request. This strip is the only instance of this type in the whole book where "que" is not used, so statistically that should tell you something about how often you can omit it.

#7 ¿Qué les parece que recolectemos ...? How does it seem to you if we collect...? The verb " parecer" in a question can trigger the subjunctive when the basic premise is up in the air, and indicates a suggestion. Will the collection take place? What do the other postmen think? Condorito is throwing this idea out in an "unsure" way. "*¿Qué le parece que vayamos a México de vacaciones?*"= " *What do you think about us going to Mexico for vacation?*" Normally a positive "parecer" sentence takes indicative: e.g. *Me parece que Juan está en la biblioteca.* A negative sentence with "parecer" will take subjunctive. *No nos parece que Miguel sea tan generoso = It doesn't seem to us that Miguel is so generous.* The verb functions like "creer" in this respect, and for that reason is included in this section.

#8 la cantidad que podamos: the quantity that we can. This type of subjunctive will be fully covered in section 6. It is used here because of the uncertainty regarding the amount. How much will they collect? In English this can be expressed by saying "whatever we manage to collect": an uncertain amount.

#11 le rogaría que ... me envíes: I would beg you to send me. Another instance of emotion/ volition subjunctive.

Quiz III: Dudar/ Parecer/ Creer

1. It doesn't seem to me that he has enough money to buy the car.

____

2. I don't doubt that they know her.

____

3. Do you believe that Phil Collins has a lot of hair???

____

4. She doesn't believe that I understand the book.

____

5. They believe that John drives well.

____

6. They doubt that he can play the game.

____

7. It seems that they are in the office today.

____

8. He doubts that we might pe able to speak Spanish well in less than a year.

____

9. Do you (really?) think that they might go to Mexico next month?

____

Section IV

Time

MEDICINA
¿Y QUÉ PUEDO HACER PARA MI ENFERMEDAD, DOCTOR?
NO TE PREOCUPES, SANARÁS PRONTO.
PARA TU DOLENCIA, TE VOY A REGALAR ESTA MEDICINA QUE TENGO AQUÍ.
GRACIAS.
20.022
PERO FÍJATE, UNGENIO, QUE ESTA MEDICINA ES SÓLO PARA USO EXTERNO.
NO SE PREOCUPE, DOCTOR. LA TOMARÉ CUANDO ESTÉ EN EL JARDÍN.
¡PLO

ESPERO QUE MAÑANA AMANEZCAS TAN BIEN COMO HOY, PEPE, PARA QUE EL DOCTOR TE DÉ DE ALTA...
POR SER MI ÚLTIMA NOCHE EN EL HOSPITAL, ¿ME PODRÍAS HACER UN FAVOR MUY ESPECIAL?
¿DE QUÉ SE TRATA, PEPE?
¡QUIERO QUE ME DES UN BESO DE BUENAS NOCHES!
16.552
¡TENDRÁS QUE ESPERAR, PEPE!
¿HASTA CUÁNDO, PRECIOSA?
¡HASTA QUE LLEGUE EL ENFERMERO QUE HACE LOS TRABAJOS PESADOS!

Medicina

vt | vi

sanar: to heal, cure | recover, get better

dolencia: pain; (here meaning medical condition). ailment, ache

fíjate: observe.

Subjunctive

#4 La tomaré cuando está en el jardín: I will take it when I'm in the yard. The first thing we notice about the subjunctive with time expressions is that we don't need a change of subject. The other main point is that we have no "que". *I will leave when I finish = Saldré cuando termine.* The word "cuando" triggers the subjunctive because it is a future action that hasn't occurred yet. The subjunctive is not used after "cuando" when the sentence expresses a generalization, because generalizations are not future oriented. *I (always) leave when I finish = Yo salgo cuando termino.* This sentence describes what the person always, or generally does. "Cuando" takes subjunctive if the sentence talks about the future. *When I see her I will give her the book = Cuando la vea le daré el libro.*

Enfermo

amanecer: to wake up. Often used in the phrase "¿Cómo amaneció?" (lit. "How did you wake up today?).

te dé de alta: releases you (from the hospital). E.g. "¡Pobre Miguel! No le van a dar de alta hasta pasado mañana."

anteayer — pasado mañana

el enfermero: the male nurse (orderly).

Subjunctive

#1 espero que amanezcas tan bien como hoy: I hope you wake up as well as today. This is an emotion/ volition subjunctive. *I hope you have luck with the exam = Espero que te vaya bien en el examen.*
She hopes we find the museum = Ella espera que encontremos el museo. Remember that in English the "that" can be dropped, but in Spanish the "que" must be used in this class of subjunctive.

#2 Quiero que me des un beso: I want you to give me a kiss. Emotion /volition subjunctive. Remember that this type needs a "que", too, even though the English version is set up differently. *He wants you to buy it = El quiere que Ud. lo compre.*

#4 hasta que llegue el enfermero: until the nurse arrives. The subjunctive is required because "hasta" has a future setting here. *We will wait until Jane calls = Vamos a esperar hasta que Jane nos llame.* Is it possible for "hasta" to not have a future connotation? Yes, if it is a generalization! *Children play until someone gets hurt = Los niños juegan hasta que alguien se hace daño.* This sentence is talking about what generally happens, or has happened. In this respect it can be said that "cuando" and "hasta que" function in the same way.

¡GLUB!
SUERTE QUE ENCONTRAMOS ESTE TRONCO. ASÍ PODREMOS MANTENERNOS A FLOTE, UNGENIO.
HACE UNA SEMANA QUE ESTAMOS FLOTANDO Y TODAVÍA NO AVISTAMOS TIERRA.
¡MORIREMOS DE HAMBRE Y SED!
¡MIRA, ALLÁ HAY UNA ISLA! ¡ESTAMOS SALVADOS!
¡RÁPIDO! NADEMOS HASTA ALLÁ ANTES QUE NOS LLEVE LA CORRIENTE PARA OTRO LADO.
¡FUERZA!
RATO DESPUÉS...
¡REFLAUTA! ¡UNGENIO SE ESTÁ HUNDIENDO!
¡GLUB! ¡GLUB!
¡GLUB!
¡UNGENIO! ¿TE ESTÁS AHOGANDO?
¡GLUB! ¡NO, SÓLO VOY A BAJAR UN RATITO A DESCANSAR! ¡GLUB!
¡PLOP!

Glub

Hace una semana que estamos flotando: We have been floating for a week. "Hace + time + que" is a very necessary construction in Spanish. *I have been studying Spanish for two years = Hace dos años que estudio español.* *She has known Fritz for six months = Hace __________ que ella ____________ a Fritz.*

avistar: to sight, catch sight of

hundiendo: sinking (hundirse).

ahogando: drowning (ahogarse).

Subjunctive

#4 Nademos hasta allá antes que nos <u>lleve</u> la corriente: Let's swim towards there before the current <u>takes</u> us away. "Antes que" (before) has a future context, and therefore requires the subjunctive. It needs a change of subject, however-- as we see here: Let <u>us</u> swim before <u>the current</u> takes us.
I want to eat before I leave for school. This sentence has the future aspect, <u>but</u> no change of subject. *Quiero comer antes de salir para la escuela.* When there is no change of subject we use the infinitive-- as if we were saying in English: *I want to eat before leaving for school.* If we have two people, then we use the subjunctive. *I want to eat before Jane arrives = Quiero comer antes de que llegue Jane.*
Seem difficult? Let's look at some more examples:
I have to turn on the computer before I start working. Will this sentence take subjunctive or not? It's true that it's future oriented, but we have the same agent on both sides of the "before". No subjunctive: rather we use the infinitive-- as if saying : *I have to turn on the computer before beginning work = Tengo que encender la computadora antes de empezar a trabajar.*
We have to finish the report before the teacher gets mad. Indicative or subjunctive?
We have different agents on either side of the "before" so the answer is subjunctive.
Tenemos que terminar el informe antes de que <u>se enoje</u> la profesora.
Don't be too concerned if this seems slightly confusing. We will see many examples of "time" subjunctive in this book; the concept will sink in.

el/la sucesor(a) = successor, heir(ess)
el/la anteccesor(a) = predecesser

Ultimo recurso = last resort

alcalde: mayor.

Sanhueza: a last name.

apurado: in a fix. ... peligrar de hacer algo

peligrar: to be in danger. Of course "está en peligro" is another way of saying this.

empeora: gets worse. This could also be expressed "se pone peor".

lincharme: ~~to hang me~~ (to lynch). me el linchamiento

Subjunctive

#3 cuando te encuentres: when you find yourself. Subjunctive is used here because it is referring to the future. "When" does not always refer to the future: *When I smoke, I always cough = Cuando yo fumo, siempre toso.*
Will this next sentence be subjunctive or indicative?
When you call Bill, remind him that the party begins at five. Is the "when" referring to every time you call Bill, or a single upcoming call? Obviously the latter! *Cuando le llames a Bill, recuérdale que la fiesta empieza a las cinco.*

#4 cuando te veas realmente apurado y peligre tu vida: when you see youself in a fix and your life is in danger. Both verbs are referring to the future after the single "cuando".
My parents will attend the ceremony when I graduate = Mis padres asistirán a la ceremonia cuando me gradúe.

PLANTA ALTA
QUE LINDO DEBE SER VOLAR, CONDORITO. NUNCA HE SUBIDO A UN AVIÓN.
6872
¿SABES, UNGENIO? TENGO UN AMIGO PILOTO. IRÉ A VER SI SE ENCUENTRA AQUÍ PARA QUE TE LLEVE A VOLAR UN RATO.
SERÍA FANTÁSTICO. TE ESPERO AQUÍ.
VUELVO LUEGO.
SU ATENCIÓN, POR FAVOR, EL SEÑOR UNGENIO GONZÁLEZ, TENGA LA AMABILIDAD DE SUBIR A LA PLANTA ALTA.
¿AH?
RATO DESPUÉS...
QUÉ CONTENTO SE VA A PONER UNGENIO CUANDO SEPA QUE MI AMIGO PILOTO LO VA A PASEAR EN AVIÓN.
SU ATENCIÓN, POR FAVOR.
?
SE RUEGA AL SEÑOR UNGENIO GONZÁLEZ QUE BAJE DE LA PALMERA...
PLOP

DESTINO
¡CHISPAS, OTRA VEZ ESTÁ BORRACHO!
¡QUIERO OLVIDAR! ¡OTRO TRAGO!
¿QUÉ TE PASA, GARGANTA?
¡AAY, CONDORITO, QUÉ DESTINO TAN TERRIBLE EL DEL HOMBRE!
¿POR QUÉ DICES ESO, GARGANTA?
¡PORQUE UNO TOMA PARA OLVIDAR A LA VIEJA QUE TIENE EN CASA...!
¡Y CUANDO UNO VUELVE LA VE DOBLE!
¡PLOP!

Planta alta

planta alta: the upper floor (also the tall plant).

Subjunctive

#2 para que te lleve a volar: so that he can take you flying. "Para que" always requires the subjunctive. The trick is that in English we can say "in order to" even with no change of subject. In Spanish you cannot.
I study in order to get good grades. This will not take "para que," and therefore will have no subjunctive. There is no change of subject so we use "para". *Yo estudio para sacar buenas notas.*
I study so that my grades improve. This will take subjunctive. The first half of the sentence is about "I" doing something, while the second half is about the grades doing something. The "subject" or "actor" on both sides of the "que" doesn't have to be a person. *Estudio para que mis notas mejoren.*

#5 cuando sepa: when he finds out. Subjunctive follows this "cuando". Remember that a change of subject is not a requirement for this type of subjunctive. Also, we do not use the "que" with "cuando". *Juan will be angry when he finds out = Juan se enojará cuando se entere.*

#7 se ruega... que baje: It's requested that he descend. This is emotion/ volition subjunctive. *I t's requestedthat people make less noise = Se ruega que las personas hagan menos ruido.*

Destino

chispas: heck (lit. sparks).

borracho: drunk.

trago: alcoholic shot.

la vieja: the wife (lit. the old lady).

Subjunctive

#4 ¡Y cuando uno vuelve la ve doble: And when one returns, he sees her double. There is no subjunctive here. The reason? This is a generalization. You drink to forget about your wife, and when you return you see her double. There is no hint of future in this sentence, or of any upcoming event.
When I go to the store I always buy coffee = Cuando voy a la tienda, siempre compro café. But let's change the sentence slightly:
When I go to the store, I will have have to get coffee. Now this sentence is about your next trip to the market. It's not a generalization. *Cuando vaya a la tienda, voy a tener que comprar café.*
= tendré

¡PERMISO! VOY A CERRAR LA VENTANILLA.
¡NO! NO QUIERO QUE LA CIERRE.
¡QUÉ SE IMAGINA, LA CIERRO Y PUNTO!
¡Y YO LA ABRO!
¡PAF!
¡DIJE QUE LA QUIERO CE-RRADAAAA!!!
¡PLAM!
¡Y YO ABIER-TAAAA!!!
¡ARRIBA!
¡ABAJO!
¿SUCEDE ALGO, SEÑO-RAS?
¡INSPECTOR, TENEMOS UN PROBLEMA!
¡NECESITO LA VENTANA ABIERTA, O SI NO ME MUERO DE ASFIXIA!
¡YO NECESITO LA VENTANA CE-RRADA, PORQUE DE LO CONTRA-RIO ME MUERO DE PULMO-NÍA!
LA COSA ES MUY SENCILLA, SEÑORAS. LES PROPONGO UN FALLO SALOMÓNICO: DEJARE-MOS LA VENTANILLA ABIER-TA...
...HASTA QUE ESTA SEÑORA MUERA DE PULMO-NÍA. ENTONCES LA CERRAMOS...
...HASTA QUE ESTA OTRA MUERA DE ASFIXIA, Y PUNTO...
¡PLOP!
¡PLOP!

la asfixia = suffocation

morir(se) de asfixia = vi. > to suffocate

Tren

¿qué se imagina?: What are you thinking?

asfixia: asphyxiation.

pulmonía: pneumonia.

fallo salomónico: a Solomonian judgement. This refers to a Biblical passage where the judge Solomon threatens to divide a baby in two in order to determine who its real mother is. The application here is that Condorito is going to do something drastic to resolve the issue.

decisión

y punto: and that's the end. Also can be expressed "y basta" or "es el sansacabose".

¡Sanseacabó!

Subjunctive

#2. No quiero que la cierre: I don't want you to close it. This is the simple emotion/ volition category.
He wants you to watch the program = El quiere que veas el programa.
Remember, if there is no change of subject, no subjunctive.
She wants to read the book = Ella quiere leer el libro.

#12 hasta que esta señora muera: until this lady dies. The hasta is pointing to a single, specific future action, so we have subjunctive after "hasta".

#13 hasta que esta otra muera: until this other dies. See previous note.

fallo >
① gen = failure, breakdown, mistake
② jur. = sentence, decision, ruling

de lo contrario = otherwise

FAVOR
¿PUEDO DECIRTE ALGO, MI AMOR?
¡POR SUPUESTO, MI AMOR!
22.102
ADMITO QUE SIEMPRE ANDES CON LAS MANOS EN LOS BOLSILLOS, QUE SILBES CUANDO MAMÁ HABLA, Y QUE EN LA MESA HABLES CON LA BOCA LLENA. PERO SÍ QUISIERA PEDIRTE UN FAVOR.
¿CUÁL?
¡QUE TE QUITES EL CIGARRILLO DE LA BOCA CADA VEZ QUE QUIERAS BESARME!
¡PLOP!

SUEÑO
¿QUÉ QUIERES SER CUANDO SEAS GRANDE, CONE?
26.786
MI SUEÑO ES GANAR TREINTA MIL PESOS AL MES, COMO MI TÍO.
¡CARACOLES! ¿TANTO GANA TU TÍO AL MES?
NO, PERO TAMBIÉN SUEÑA CON ESO.
¡PLOP!

admitir = admit, accept, allow (for), leave room for (dudas, etc.)

Favor

admito: I allow, I put up with.

silbar: to whistle. The verb "chiflar" is also used in some countries.

Subjunctive

#2 admito que andes: I put up with you walking. This is emotion/ volition subjunctive.
I don't put up with students smoking in my class = No admito que los alumnos fumen en mi clase.

#2 (admito) que silbes: (I put up with) you whistling. It's not necessary to repeat the trigger verb " admito". The subjunctive still must follow.

#2 (admito) que en la mesa hables: that you talk. See previous two notes.

#3 (pedirte) que te quites el cigarrillo: (ask you) that you remove the cigarette. The trigger is "pedir" from the previous box. This is emotion/ volition subjunctive.
I ask you to think it over well = Te pido que lo pienses bien.

#3 cada vez que quieras besarme: every time that you want to kiss me. "Cada vez" here implies every time from now on-- so it will take the subjunctive. However, if "cada vez" suggests a generalization or habit, there will be no subjunctive:
The librarian helps me every time that I go to the library = La bibliotecaria me ayuda cada vez que voy a la biblioteca.

Sueño

sueño: dream (desire or ambition here). soñar con

caracoles: gosh (lit. snails).

sueña con: he dreams about. ¿Con qué soñaste anoche? = What did you dream about last night?

Subjunctive

#1 cuando seas grande: when you are big. This "cuando" refers to a future state, and is not a generalization. Subjunctive is required.

La FOTO
3.419-
¡HOLA, CONDORITO, ¿A DÓNDE VAS?
¡VOY A ENTREGAR UNAS HORTALIZAS AL PUEBLO, HUEVODURO.
¿HAS TENIDO NOTICIAS DE YAYITA, QUE ESTÁ EN LA CAPITAL?
¡SÍ, HUEVO, PRECISAMENTE APROVECHARÉ DE TOMARME UNA FOTO Y SE LA ENVIARÉ PARA QUE NO ME OLVIDE!
¡DALE MIS SALUDOS, CONDORITO!
¡GRACIAS, HUEVO! ¡HASTA LA VISTA!
HORAS DESPUÉS...
POR FIN LLEGAMOS A PELOTILLEHUE, "MANDÍBULA".
AL RATO...
MISIÓN CUMPLIDA. LAS HORTALIZAS, VENDIDAS... "MANDÍBULA" COMIENDO... Y AHORA A TOMARME UNA FOTO PARA YAYITA...
SACA BUENAS FOTOS, POR LO QUE SE VE...
¿LE TOMO UNA FOTO, AMIGO?
¿QUIÉN DIJO MIEDO? SÁQUEME UNA DE CUERPO ENTERO...
¿LISTO, SEÑOR? SONRÍA... ¡OIGA, PERO!... ¿QUÉ ESTÁ HACIENDO?
¡SALGA DE AHÍ, SEÑOR!
¡TÓMELA ASÍ NO MÁS, LE DIGO!
CUANDO LA RECIBA YAYITA, YO APAREZCO DETRÁS DEL ÁRBOL Y LE DOY LA GRAN SORPRESA...
¡PLOP!

misión cumplida = "mission accomplished"

La foto

hortalizas: vegetables., specifically "garden produce"

+ de

aprovecharé: I will take advantage (of something or somebody).

Mandíbula: Condorito's horse (lit. Jawbone).

Subjunctive

#2 Enviaré... para que no me olvide: I will send her (a photo) so that she doesn't forget me. A straightforward use of "para que".
Remember "para que" always needs two agents. "I go to the library in order to look for books" must be said "Voy a la biblioteca para buscar libros" since there is only one actor -- yo-- in the sentence.

#10 cuando la reciba Yayita: When Yayita receives it. This "cuando" is pointing to a specific, single future action, so subjunctive is mandatory. Remember that if it is a generalization, it will be indicative:
When I go to that restaurant, I always order soup = Cuando yo voy a ese restaurante, siempre pido sopa.

por lo que se ve = based on how it/he/she looks

¿quién dijo miedo? = what's to be afraid of?

no más = just

Quiz IV: Time

1. When I graduate I want to find a job in Mexico.

___

2. I will stay at home until Jane calls.

___

3. We have to finish the composition before the professor returns.

___

4. When I work too hard I get tired.

___

5. Every time (from now on) that you arrive late, you will receive a fine.

___

6. We will begin the project after John arrives.

___

7. As soon as we finish we have to leave.

___

8. Children (always) fight until someone gets hurt.

___

9. The students can't go home until the teacher tells them so.

___

10. When you come to Chicago, please don't forget to visit me.

___

11. As soon as I find out about it, I will let you know.

___

Section V

Negation

CARTA
AHÍ VIENE LA SEÑORITA YAYITA.
¿CUÁNTAS CARTAS TRAERÁ ESTA VEZ?
HACE CARTAS PARA TODO.
15.829
NIÑOS, QUIERO QUE LES ENTREGUEN ESTAS CARTAS A SUS PADRES. EN ELLAS LES INFORMO SOBRE LAS ÚLTIMAS ACTIVIDADES DE LA ESCUELA.
¿NO TE DIJE? NO HAY DÍA EN QUE NO MANDE UNA CARTA ESTA PRO-FESORA.
SEÑORITA YAYITA...
DIME, PEDRITO.
TENGO UNA NUEVA HERMANITA.
¡PERO QUÉ NOTICIA, PEDRITO!
VOY A ESCRIBIRLE UNA CARTA A TU MAMÁ.
NO SE MOLESTE, SEÑORITA.
ELLA YA LO SABE.
¡PLOP!

Carta

¿Cuántas cartas traerá?: How many letters do you suppose she's carrying? Remember that the future sometimes means probability.
Ella tendrá treinta años = She must be about thirty.

Subjunctive

#2 quiero que les entreguen estas cartas a sus padres: I want you to deliver these letters to your parents. Emotion/ volition subjunctive.

#3 No hay día en que no mande una carta: There is no day that she doesn't send a letter. Here we see the subjunctive of absolute negation. *There is not a person in this room who can explain it = No hay nadie en esta clase que pueda explicarlo.*
There's no book in the library that contains that information = No hay ningún libro en la biblioteca que contenga esa información.
Sentences of this type often begin with "no hay".
There's no teacher that knows how to explain it = No hay profesor que sepa explicarlo.
Obviously a sentence like *There's nobody in the gym* will not take subjunctive, because there is no verb following "no hay". *No hay nadie en el gimnasio.*

CRIADO
24.164
ENTONCES, DESDE HOY, USTED TRABAJARÁ PARA MÍ.
SÍ, SEÑORA.
PERO ME GUSTARÍA HACERLE UNA PREGUNTA.
PREGUNTE LO QUE DESEE, SEÑORA.
SUPONGO QUE USTED NO SERÁ DE ESOS CRIADOS A LOS QUE HAY QUE LLAMAR UNAS VEINTE VECES POR LA MAÑANA.
¡AL CONTRARIO, NO HAY NADA QUE ME MOLESTE TANTO COMO ESO...!
¡PLOP!

MANO
CONDORITO, CREO QUE USTED ES DEMASIADO ATREVIDO.
¿POR QUÉ ME DICE ESO, SEÑORITA?
¿QUE NO SE DA CUENTA? HAGA FAVOR DE SOLTARME LA MANO.
¡PERO SI NO TIENE NADA DE MALO QUE YO LE TOME LA MANO!
¿Y QUÉ DIRÍA MI MAMÁ SI NOS VIERA?
¡LE PODEMOS DECIR QUE SOY SU HERMANO!
¡PLOP!

Criado

desde hoy: from today on.

criado: servant.

Subjunctive

#2 pregunte lo que desee: Ask what(ever) you wish. This type of subjunctive will be fully covered in the next section. For now, the subjunctive appears here because the idea of "whatever you wish" is up in the air.

#4 No hay nada que me moleste como eso: There is nothing that bothers me like that. Here is a subjunctive of the absolute negation type. As previously seen, it begins with "no hay".
There is no-one that I like = No hay nadie que me guste.
There are no buts about it = No hay pero que valga.

Mano

demasiado: too (excessive).

¿Que no se da cuenta?: You don't realize? "Darse cuenta" is a common expression in Spanish. *I realize the situation is difficult = Me doy cuenta de que la situación es difícil.*

Subjunctive

#3 No tiene nada de malo que yo le tome la mano: There is nothing wrong with me taking your hand. The negation here is obvious. While it doesn't begin with "no hay" the negation is still total.

Apuro

prestar: to lend

no es que la tome: It's not that I take you. "It's not that" always forms a complete negation, and always requires subjunctive. Memorize this one!
No es que ...(subj) , sino que ... (indic.)
It's not that I don't like music, but I have no time to practice =No es que no me guste la música, sino que no tengo tiempo para practicar.
It's not that Joe spends so much money, but rather that his car consumes too much gas =No es que Joe gaste tanto dinero, sino que su coche consume demasiado combustible.

Quiz V : Negation

1. There isn't a day that the teacher doesn't arrive early.

____

2. There is nothing in the book that clarifies the concept.

____

3. There is nothing wrong with us borrowing the jacket.

____

4. It's not that the book is difficult; rather that it is long.

____

5. I see no-one that has the book.

____

6. There isn't anybody that knows where the key is.

____

Section VI

Indefinite

COW BOY
8.777
VEN PARA ACÁ, PRECIOSURA.
¡ESTE HOMBRE ME ESTÁ MOLESTANDO!..
... ¡NI SIQUIERA LO CONOZCO!... ¿NO HAY POR AQUÍ UN CABALLERO QUE PONGA LAS COSAS EN SU LUGAR?
¡HEY, TÚ!... ¿CÓMO TE LLAMAS?
¡JUAN EL RUDO!
SEÑORITA, TENGO EL HONOR DE PRESENTARLE A JUAN EL RUDO, AHORA LO CONOCE.
¡PLOP!

Cowboy

preciosura: honey, sweetie.

ni siquiera: (I) don't even.

caballero: gentleman.

Subjunctive

#3 No hay por aquí un caballero que ponga ?: Is there no gentleman here who will put...? The subjunctive here is required because the situation is very indefinite. This sentence is similar to the negation type seen in the last section. Here it is not complete negation because the possibility is open, however. The sentence *There is no gentleman here who will help me* would be subjunctive of the negative type: *No hay ningún caballero aquí que me ayude.* Indefiniteness can be best expressed by looking at a want ad:
I need a secretary that speaks French. This secretary may or may not be found. What we mean is "I need some secretary-- one that would speak French.
Necesito un secretario que hable francés.
This is the very type of subjunctive we see in this frame of Condorito: *Is there no gentleman here who can help me?*

CONDORITO
ZAPATERIA
CALZADO EXCLUSIVO PARA DAMAS
OH, VIENE ENTRANDO UN MONUMENTO.
SEÑORA, ¿EN QUÉ PUEDO SERVIRLE?
QUISIERA UN PAR DE ZAPATOS QUE HAGA JUEGO CON UN VESTIDO DE BAILE ELEGANTE Y MUY ESCOTADO.
INMEDIATAMENTE, SEÑORA, TOME ASIENTO.
AQUÍ LE TENGO EL PRECISC...
NO, NO ME AGRADA...
LE BUSCARÉ ALGO QUE LA VA A DEJAR CONTENTA.
OBSERVE QUÉ MARAVILLA.
RATO DESPUÉS...
ES TODO LO QUE TENEMOS, SEÑORA...
QUÉ LÁSTIMA. NINGUNO HACE JUEGO CON MI VESTIDO DE BAILE.
NO SE PREOCUPE POR ESO, SEÑORA. SI SU VESTIDO DE BAILE ES TAN ESCOTADO COMO USTED DICE, ¿CREE QUE HABRÁ ALGÚN ESTÚPIDO QUE VA A MIRARLE LOS ZAPATOS?...
¡EXIJO UNA EXPLICACIÓN!

Zapatería

hacer juego: to match.

escotado: low-cut.

Subjunctive

#4 un par de zapatos que haga juego con un vestido: a pair of shoes that match a dress.
The indefinite subjunctive is called for here. She doesn't have a specific pair of shoes in mind, she needs a pair that will combine with her dress.
However, if we say:
I have a shirt that matches this sportcoat, in this case the shirt is specific and real, so we will say *Tengo una camisa que hace juego con este saco.*
What happens if we say *I'm looking for a shirt that matches these pants* ?
This would be "up in the air", and would take subjunctive: *Busco una camisa que haga juego con estos pantalones.*
Buscar, necesitar, and querer are verbs that often trigger this type of subjunctive.

#6 Le buscaré algo que le va a dejar contenta: I will look for something that will leave you satisfied. There is no subjunctive here, because Condorito has the specific pair in mind. He knows just what he's going to get her from the storeroom. It turns out she doesn't like them, but he thought she would be happy with them.

¡IDENTIDAD!
7604
¡HOLA, CONDORITO! ¿ADÓNDE VAS TAN CONTENTO?
A COBRAR UN CHEQUE AL BANCO. ACOMPÁÑAME, COMEGATO.
YA LLEGAMOS.
BANCO DE PELOTILLEH
PÁGUEME ESTE CHEQUE POR FAVOR.
SU CARNET, SEÑOR.
CAJA 2
NO LO TENGO, SEÑOR.
NO PUEDO PAGARLE ESTE CHEQUE HASTA QUE TRAIGA UN DOCUMENTO QUE LO IDENTIFIQUE.
¡OH! NO SE PREOCUPE POR ESO. MI AMIGO COMEGATO ME IDENTIFICARÁ.
CAJA 2
PERO ES QUE YO TAMPOCO CONOZCO AL SEÑOR COMEGATO.
DISCULPE. ¡QUÉ DISTRAÍDO SOY! ¡OLVIDÉ PRESENTARLOS!
¡PLOP!

Identidad

cobrar: to cash (usu. means to charge).

carnet: I.D. card (already seen).

Comegato: Condorito's friend.

Subjunctive

#4 hasta que traiga un documento: until you bring a document. We see a "time" type of subjunctive here, as previously covered. The "hasta que" here points to the future, and is not a generalization, so we need the subjunctive.
Little babies cry until someone feeds them = Las criaturas lloran hasta que alguien les da de comer. This is a generalization, so there is no subjunctive. However: *I'm going to pester Jane until she lends me the book* has the idea of a specific upcoming action or goal. *Voy a importunarle hasta que me preste el libro.*

#4 un documento que lo identifique : a document that identifies you. Here we see the indefinite subjunctive. The clerk wants to see any document that would identify Condorito.
If you say *I have a document that identifies me* the sentence will be indicative, because you are referring to a specific, known document: *Tengo un documento que me identifica.*
What are some common triggers for indefinite subjunctive? Verbs like buscar, necesitar, querer.
I want an apartment that has a balcony = Quiero un apartamento que tenga un balcón. = I want some apartment that would have a balcony.

CONDORITO
TRA-LARÁ-LARÁ LARÁ...
PÁJAROS Y ANIMALES DOMÉSTICOS
¿CÓMO HAN AMANECIDO, MIS QUERIDOS ANIMALITOS?
AHÍ LLEGA LA PRIMERA CLIENTE DE LA MAÑANA.
BUENOS DÍAS, SEÑORA, ¿EN QUÉ LA PUEDO SERVIR?
MIRE, JOVEN, MI MARIDO SE HA IDO A EUROPA EN VIAJE DE NEGOCIOS POR UN AÑO... USTED COMPRENDERÁ QUE ME VOY A SENTIR MUY SOLA...
QUIERO TENER UN ANIMALITO QUE ME HAGA COMPAÑÍA...
¡HUMM! UN ANIMALITO...
SEÑORA, CON UN ANIMALITO NO HARÁ USTED NADA... POR LO MENOS NECESITARÁ TRES.
¿TRES? NO COMPRENDO.
MIRE, UN PERRO PARA QUE LE LADRE DURANTE TODO EL DÍA...
¡GRRR!
UN LORO, QUE DIGA PALABROTAS DURANTE TODO EL DÍA TAMBIÉN...
... Y UN GATO QUE SE LO PASE TODAS LAS NOCHES FUERA DE SU CASA...
¡EXIJO UNA EXPLICACIÓN!

Animales

animales domésticos: pets.

¿Cómo han amanecido?: How did you wake up today?

ladrar: to bark.

palabrotas: swear words.

Subjunctive

#5 Quiero tener un animal que me haga compañía: I want an animal that will keep me company. The animal is indefinite-- some animal-- so subjunctive is required.
But: *I want a book by Steinbeck that deals with a man named Doc who lives in a fishing village* is about a specific book. Perhaps you can't recall the title, but it is a single specific work, and would take indicative. "*Quiero el libro por Steinbeck que trata de un tal Doc que vive en un pueblito pesquero.*"

#7 un perro para que le ladre: a dog to bark for you. The subjunctive is triggered by "para que." "Para que" always takes subjunctive.

#8 (Necesita) un loro que diga palabrotas: (You need) a parrot that says swear words. This is indefinite; the trigger--necesita--appears a few frames before.

#9 (necesita) un gato que se lo pase todas las noches: (you need) a cat to spend every night out. Same as #8.

CONDORITO
Hoy Examen Escrito
¡REFLANTA! ESTOY COLGADO COMO AMPOLLETA.
YA LO SABEN. EL ALUMNO QUE SALGA REPROBADO NO PODRÁ INTEGRAR EL EQUIPO DE FÚTBOL PARA LA FINAL DEL DOMINGO.
YA SÉ. ME SENTARÉ AL LADO DEL MEJOR ALUMNO PARA NO FRACASAR.
AL DÍA SIGUIENTE...
UN SOLO ALUMNO REPROBADO EN TODO EL CURSO: ¡CONDORITO!
¿QUÉ HAREMOS SIN EL CRACK MÁXIMO DEL FÚTBOL ESCOLAR?
CONDORITO ES EL CRÉDITO DEL EQUIPO.
SIN ÉL PERDEREMOS EL CAMPEONATO.
NO PUEDE SER. HABLAREMOS CON EL RECTOR.
RATO DESPUÉS...
DÍGALE AL PROFESOR Y AL ALUMNO CONDORITO QUE VENGAN A MI OFICINA.
RECTOR
ME VI OBLIGADO A PONERLE UN CERO PORQUE HIZO TRAMPA, SEÑOR RECTOR.
¿HIZO TRAMPA? ¿LO VIO USTED?
RECTOR
¡NO, NO LO VI!
¿CONFIESA ÉL HABER HECHO TRAMPA?
NO. LO NIEGA. PERO ÉL ES UN MAL ESTUDIANTE. SE SENTÓ AL LADO DEL MEJOR ALUMNO DE LA CLASE Y AMBOS ESCRIBIERON CASI LAS MISMAS RESPUESTAS...
¿CREE USTED QUE ESO ES PRUEBA DE ALGO?
EN ESTE CASO, SÍ. EL ALUMNO APROVECHADO CONTESTÓ A LA ÚLTIMA PREGUNTA: "NO SÉ LA RESPUESTA"...
Y ÉL ESCRIBIÓ: "YO TAMPOCO".
¡PLOP!

Examen

estoy colgado como ampolleta: I don't understand anything (slang).

integrar: to join.

fracasar: to fail.

reprobado: failed.

crack: star . This is borrowed from English slang of many years ago.

hizo trampa: he cheated. "Hacer trampa(s)" is to cheat in an scholastic sense. "The butcher cheated me", however, would be "El carnicero me estafó" from the verb "estafar", meaning to swindle.

Subjunctive

#2 El alumno que salga reprobado: the student who fails. This is indefinite, because no-one has taken the test yet. He means any student who fails: an up-in-the-air quantity.
The student who finishes the test first will receive an A = El estudiante que termine el examen primero sacará una A.

#6 dígale que vengan : tell him that they should come. This is emotion/ volition with the common trigger "decir".

CONSEJO
8.519
¡CONDORITO, HEMOS TERMINADO! ¡NO QUIERO VOLVER A VERTE!
¿AH, SÍ? ¡MIRA QUE COINCIDENCIA, YO TAMPOCO PIENSO VERTE MÁS!
¡MAL AGRADECIDA! ¡Y YO QUE PENSABA CASARME CON ELLA!...
... ¡JUNTANDO DINERO PARA COMPRAR MUEBLES, EL MUY TONTO!...
... ¡PERO AHORA SÍ QUE NO LA VEO NUNCA MÁS!... ¡NO, SEÑOR!...
¡PAF!
... ¡POR LO MENOS, YO NO PIENSO HACER NADA PARA VOLVER CON ELLA!...
POBRE... ESTÁ HABLANDO SOLO.
... ¡SI QUIERE VOLVER CONMIGO VA A SER ELLA LA QUE SE HUMILLE ESTA VEZ! ¡NO ESTOY HABLANDO SOLO, NO, SEÑOR!...
... ¡ESTA VEZ VA A SER ELLA LA QUE ME VA A ROGAR!
¿QUÉ QUIERES?
¡TOC! ¡TOC!
NADA... ¡SÓLO QUERÍA DECIRTE QUE SI QUIERES VOLVER CONMIGO, VAS A SER TÚ LA QUE TENGA QUE TOMAR LA INICIATIVA!
¡PLOP!

Consejo

volver a verte: see you again. "Volver a + infinitive" is a common expression. "Volví a leer el libro" (I read the book again).

mal agradecida(o): ungrateful.

el muy tonto: What a big idiot.

Subjunctive

#6 va a ser ella la que se humille : It's going to be her that gets humiliated. Indefinite subjunctive, because this is all seen as potential. If she decides to apologize, then she will be the one to be humiliated.

#7 va a ser ella la que me va a rogar: It's going to be her that is going to beg me. Indicative this time, simply because he's looking at this possibility with more certainty, more confidence. The verb itself "ir" won't tend to take subjunctive in this setting, as it has a hue of certainty about it that other verbs don't. Without the verb "ir" this sentence would come out as subjunctive: "va a ser ella la que me ruegue ".

#9 vas a ser tú la que tenga que tomar la iniciativa: It's going to be you that has to take the initiative. Here we have a return to the subjunctive. He's a little intimidated by speaking to her face-to-face, so he's putting this proposition to her in the more "potential" subjunctive.

Quiz VI: Indefinite

1. Is there a book here that explains the subjunctive?

____

2. (At the pet shop) I'm looking for a cat that has a nice personality.

____

3. Maybe he can suggest something that can help us.

____

4. Do you have a document that identifies you?

____

5. I want to buy a dog that doesn't bark.

____

6. I need a pen that writes in 3 colors.

____

7. The first who finishs will collect the papers.

____

8. Whoever speaks a foreign language, please stand up.

____

9. He is looking for a tie that matches his jacket.

____

Section VII

Present Perfect

CONDORITO
FELICÍTEME, CUMPA. ME SAQUÉ CINCO MIL PESOS, EN LA LOTERÍA.
ME ALEGRO, COMPADRE. QUE LE DUREN.
LE ACONSEJO QUE ABRA UNA CUENTA EN EL BANCO, COMPADRE. NO CONVIENE GUARDAR LA PLATA DEBAJO DEL COLCHÓN.
¿CÓMO ES LA COSA?
MUY SENCILLA. USTED DEPOSITA LOS CINCO MIL PESOS EN EL BANCO, LE DAN UN TALONARIO Y USTED HACE SUS PAGOS CON CHEQUES.
ACOMPÁÑEME, CUMPA.
BANCO
¿DE CUÁNTAS HOJAS LE DAMOS EL LIBRETO DE CHEQUES?
DE LOS MÁS GORDOS. DE CIEN HOJAS.
¿VIO QUE SENCILLO?
VOY COMPRENDIENDO. PERO ¿ESTARÁ SEGURA MI PLATA ALLÁ ADENTRO?
UN TIEMPO DESPUÉS...
CARTA DEL BANCO.
...Y LE ROGAMOS PASAR A LA BREVEDAD POSIBLE POR NUESTRA SECCIÓN "CUENTAS CORRIENTES".
¡ADELANTE!
JEFE CUENTAS CORRIENTES
SEÑOR, USTED ESTÁ SOBREGIRADO EN SU CUENTA Y TIENE QUE CUBRIR EL EXCEDENTE.
¡CÓMO ES POSIBLE QUE SE ME HAYA ACABADO LA PLATA, SI RECIÉN VOY EN LA MITAD DEL LIBRETO!
¡PLOP!

Bank

una cuenta: an account.

no conviene: it's not suitable.

plata: money. This word is used often in spoken Spanish.

colchón: mattress.

talonario: checkbook.

a la brevedad posible: as soon as possible.

sobregirado: overdrawn.

Subjunctive

#1 que le duren: may they last you. This is a common type of subjunctive where tha verb of emotion (I hope/ I wish) is omitted. *(I hope) you have a good weekend= que pases un buen fin de semana.*

#2 Le aconsejo que abra: I advise you to open. Emotion/ volition.

#8 Le rogamos pasar: We beg you to pass by. There is no subjunctive here, and yet there should be, according to all the rules we've seen. The answer is that there could be subjunctive here. *Le rogamos que pase* is an excellent sentence. Why do they use the infinitive in the letter? There are a handful of verbs that can take the infinitive in this way--BUT THEY NEVER HAVE TO. The verbs in question are hacer, rogar and dejar. The best advice to the student is to use the subjunctive with these verbs, as it is always perfectly correct. If you choose to try the infinitive alternative, remember--only do it with these select 3 verbs. *I want her to study* --for example-- can only be done with the subjunctive. Scout's honor! *Quiero que ella estudie.*

For those intrepid students that want variety in their grammatical diet here's one that can go either way: *The teacher makes us study a lot.*
El profe nos hace estudiar mucho. OR *El profe hace que estudiemos mucho.*

#11 ¿es posible que se me haya acabado la plata?: is it possible that I have run out of money? This new section is about the present perfect subjunctive. "Es posible que" always takes subjunctive. Here we have the helping verb "has" in the subjunctive. *I hope he has studied.* This sentence requires the subjunctive: not ha estudiado but haya estudiado. *Espero que haya estudiado.*
We can use present perfect subjunctive after the category of dudar / creer, as well. *She doesn't believe that I have read the book = Ella no cree que yo haya leído el libro.*

ESQUELETO
¡CHISPAS! ES DE NO CREER.
20,047
VE A ESE CHAVO. ¡SE QUEDÓ HELADO!
PARECE QUE EL ESQUELETO LE LLAMÓ LA ATENCIÓN.
¿QUÉ PASA, HIJO? ¿NO PUEDES CREER QUE HAYA EXISTIDO UNA COSA ASÍ?
¡LO QUE ME ASOMBRA ES OTRA COSA!
¿SE LO COMIERON USTEDES SOLOS?
¡PLOP!

¡HOLA, YAYITA! ¿CÓMO ESTÁS, EH?
YO ESTOY MUY BIEN, CHOLY. ¡TÚ SÍ ESTÁS UN POCO MÁS GORDA!
¡CLARO, NIÑA! POR ESO VINE A ESTE SUPERMERCADO. ME DIJERON QUE AQUÍ VENDEN PRODUCTOS ALIMENTICIOS QUE NO HACEN ENGORDAR...
¿Y TÚ QUE HACES PARA MANTENERTE TAN ESBELTA?
BUENO, CHOLY, YO NUNCA COMO ALIMENTOS QUE TENGAN ADITIVOS O CONSERVADORES...
...ADEMÁS DE ESO, NO COMO HARINAS NI NADA QUE HAYA SIDO ROCIADO O CULTIVADO CON PRODUCTOS QUÍMICOS.
¡PERO QUÉ MARAVILLA, YAYITA! ¿Y CÓMO TE SIENTES?
¡HAMBRIENTA!
¡PLOP!

Esqueleto

helado: chilled.

le llamó la atención: it captured his interest.

asombrar: to startle.

se lo comieron: you ate it up. The reflexive with beber and comer lends the idea of eating up or guzzling down. "Se bebió toda la Pepsi."

Subjunctive

#2 No puedes creer que haya existido: you can't believe that it has existed. The trigger for subjunctive is "no creer". To believe in the affirmative doesn't take subjunctive.
We believe she has studied German = Creemos que ella ha estudiado alemán.
They don't believe that she has called = No creen que ella haya llamado.

Supermercado

estás gorda: you look fat.

esbelta: slender.

conservadores: preservatives.

harinas: flours.

rociado: sprayed (rociar).

Subjunctive

#3 alimentos que tengan aditivos: foods that have additives. This is the indefinite subjunctive.
The idea is "I never eat any foods that...-- not a specific real food.

#4 ni nada que haya sido rociado: nor anything that has been sprayed. This is the subjunctive of negation.
There is no-one who can live without breathing = No hay nadie que pueda vivir sin respirar.

BESOS
¡REFLAUTA! ¿Y CÓMO HAGO AHORA? ¿CÓMO SE LO EXPLICO A YAYITA...?
23.537
ESPERO QUE NO LO TOME A MAL Y SE TERMINE TODO LO NUESTRO.
¡CONDORITO, QUÉ BUENO QUE HAYAS VENIDO; TENÍA TANTAS GANAS DE VERTE!
¡HOLA, YAYITA!
¿QUÉ TE SUCEDE, CONDORITO? TE NOTO MUY RARO.
ESTE... TENGO QUE DECIRTE ALGO MUY SERIO, YAYITA.
¿QUÉ, CONDORITO?
¡GLUB! ANOCHE, EN LA FIESTA, BESÉ A UNA NIÑA CREYENDO QUE ERAS TÚ.
¡NO TE PREOCUPES, CONDORITO, PORQUE ANOCHE EN LA FIESTA...
...¡YO TE BESÉ, CREYENDO QUE NO ERAS TÚ...!
¡PLOP!

Besos

tomar a mal: to take it bad.

tenía tantas ganas de verte: I so wanted to see you.

te noto: You seem to me.

niña: girl (not child). In some countries "niña" is used to refer to women even through their twenties.

Subjunctive

#2 espero que no lo tome a mal: I hope she doesn't take it bad. Emotion/ volition subjunctive.

#3 Qué bueno que hayas venido: How nice that you've come. This is emotion/ volition triggering present perfect subjunctive.
It's sad that he's lost his dog = Es triste que haya perdido su perro.

FECHA
¡HOLA, CONDORITO! ¿CÓMO TE VA?
14.622
MAL, TOMATE.
¿POR QUÉ ESTÁS TAN ENOJADO?
YAYITA SE DISGUSTÓ CONMIGO PORQUE ME VIO DÁNDOLE EL ABRAZO DE AÑO NUEVO A ROSITA.
¡ESO ES LO MÁS NATURAL! ¿CÓMO ES POSIBLE QUE SE HAYA ENOJADO POR ESO?
¡TODO FUE PORQUE ERA 12 DE OCTUBRE, TOMATE!
¡PLOP!

Fecha

abrazo: hug

Subjunctive

#4 ¿Cómo es posible que se haya enojado?: How is it possible for her to have gotten mad? The trigger is "es posible". "No es posible" will also take subjunctive.
"Es posible" does need subjunctive, but it can be present perfect or simple present subjunctive.
It's not possible for me to take the exam = No es posible que tome el examen.
It's possible that he has gotten lost = Es posible que se haya perdido.
What specific triggers can give us present perfect subjunctive?
Esperar
Dudar/ no creer
Temer
Impersonal expressions, such as: es imposible; es extraño; es una lástima; ojalá; qué vergüenza, etc.

It's strange that she hasn't read the article yet = Es extraño que ella todavía no haya leído el artículo.
Of course these same impersonal expressions can give us straight present subjunctive, too.
It's strange that she wants to buy that old car = Es extraño que ella quiera comprar ese carro viejo.
I'm afraid he hasn't even bought the book = Temo que ni siquiera haya comprado el libro.

Quiz VII: Present Perfect

1. I hope that she has bought the bread.

____

2. It doesn't seem that they have studied much.

____

3. They don't believe we have seen the movie.

____

4. It's impossible for John to have finished the book so fast.

____

5. It's to be hoped for that they haven't sent the letter yet.

____

6. It's strange that you haven't tried to finish the composition.

____

7. Probably they haven't returned the books yet.

____

8. It's foolish that she hasn't bought her ticket yet.

____

9. He's really sorry that you (plural) arrived late.

____

10. Is there anyone in the room who hasn't understood the teacher?

____

11. I'm afraid the dog has eaten the cake.

____

Section VIII

Past Subjunctive

OBEDIENTE
¡CONÉ, VEN ACÁ, POR FAVOR!
YA VOY, TÍO.
8.541
YO VOY A COMPRAR ALGUNAS COSAS PARA QUE TOMEMOS TÉ, Y MIENTRAS QUIERO QUE TE FIJES CUANDO LA LECHE HIERVA. ¿ENTENDIDO?
ESTÁ BIEN, TÍO.
PERO FÍJATE CUANDO HIERVA.
¡SÍ, TÍO, ANDA TRANQUILO!
¡PERO QUÉ ES ESTO! ¡TE DIJE QUE TE FIJARAS CUANDO HIRVIERA! ¿O NO?
SÍ...
...Y ME FIJÉ... ¡SEGÚN TU RELOJ HIRVIÓ EXACTAMENTE A LAS 6:25 DE LA TARDE!
¡PLOP!

Obediente

fijarse: to notice.

hervir: to boil.

Subjunctive

#2 voy a comprar... para que tomemos té: I'm going to buy... so that we can have tea. Remember, "para que" always takes subjunctive.

#2 quiero que te fijes: I want you to notice. Simple emotion/ volition.

#2 cuando la leche hierva : when the milk boils. The "cuando" here is pointing toward the future, so the subjunctive is required.

#3 fíjate cuando hierva: Notice when it boils. See previous note.

#8 te dije que te fijaras cuando hirviera : I told you to notice when the milk boiled. Here we have 2 verbs in the past subjunctive. Any of the triggers we have seen thus far will also take subjunctive in the past. Here we see "decir" causing subjunctive, since it is an indirect command.
In the present we can say *I tell you to open the door = Te digo que abras la puerta.*
This sentence will also take the subjunctive if it is set in the past:
I told you to open the door.
We see the same uncertainty about the door opening here as we see in the present tense sentence. Did the person open the door or not? We don't know. Therefore it will be *Te dije que abrieras la puerta.* This is true of all the sentences we have seen so far. Just because a sentence is in the past doesn't mean it's indicative.
I wanted her to buy the book. This must take subjunctive, just as the present tense version would. *Yo quería que ella comprara el libro.*
Now we must examine the "cuando hirviera" part. The "cuando" was talking about a future point--not a generalization. It must take past subjunctive, because at the time of the original utterance it was regarding a future action.

PROHIBICIÓN
¡PERO GARGANTA, QUÉ TERRIBLE ERES!...¿CUÁNDO LE VAS A OBEDECER AL MÉDICO?
¿POR QUÉ ME DICES ESO, VIEJA?
19.224
¿ACASO NO TE PROHIBIÓ EL MÉDICO QUE TOMARAS VINO CON LAS COMIDAS?
POS, NI MODO... ¡LLÉVATE LA COMIDA!...
¡PLOP!

8.732
LUEGO...
¿QUÉ FUE DEL PASTEL QUE ESTABA SOBRE LA MESA?
TEMÍ QUE LAS MOSCAS SE LO COMIERAN Y LO GUARDÉ.
¿DÓNDE?
AQUÍ DENTRO. EN EL ESTÓMAGO.
¡PLOP!

Prohibición

pos = pues.

ni modo: no way.

Subjunctive

#3 te prohibió el médico que tomaras vino: the doctor forbade you to drink wine. Past subjunctive of the emotion/ volition type. As previously stated, any trigger that we have seen will also cause past subjunctive. It's just that simple! *She forbade me to open the window = Ella me prohibió que abriera la ventana.*

I asked them to buy the newspaper = Les pedí que compraran el periódico.

Queque

pastel: cake.

moscas: flies.

Subjunctive

#4 Temí que las moscas se lo comieran : I was afraid that the flies would eat it up. Again we see emotion/ volition at work here. Temer (or "tener miedo") is the trigger. Of course this trigger will work for present subjunctive, and present perfect, too.
I fear she has forgotten the notebook = Temo que ella haya olvidado el cuaderno.

HORARIO
¿ALGUIEN SABE QUÉ HORA ES?
NO, PERO TODAVÍA NO SON LAS CINCO.
¿Y TÚ CÓMO LO SABES?
¡ES CIERTO! NO TIENES RELOJ.
¡ES QUE MI PAPÁ ME DIJO QUE VOLVIERA A LAS CINCO Y TODAVÍA ESTOY AQUÍ!
¡PLOP!

ACTO
¡GRACIAS POR INVITARME A ESTA FUNCIÓN, CUMPA!
¡ME PARECIÓ QUE LA OBRA ERA INTERESANTE Y NO QUISE QUE SE LA PERDIERA.
15.721
MÁS TARDE...
BUENO, SI QUIERE, QUÉDESE, PERO YO ME VOY.
FALTA EL TERCER ACTO, QUE ES EL ÚLTIMO Y EL MÁS INTERESANTE.
¡YO ESTE AÑO TENGO MUCHO QUE HACER!
PERO ESO... ¿QUÉ TIENE QUE VER?
¡AQUÍ DICE: "TERCER ACTO, UN AÑO DESPUÉS"!
¡PLOP!

Horario

Subjunctive

#4 me dijo que volviera a las cinco. He told me to return at five. Emotion/ volition subjunctive in the past, triggered by decir.

Acto

gracias por: thanks for.

Subjunctive

#1 no quise que se la perdiera: I didn't want you to miss it. Emotion/ volition in the past, triggered by querer.
But *I wanted to read the poem = Yo quería leer el poema* is not subjunctive because there is no change of subject.
Bill wanted me to read the poem--Subjunctive! *Bill quería que yo leyera el poema.*

LA GIOCONDA
MAESTRO, ¿CUÁL ES SU ÚLTIMA OBRA?
MI AMIGO, MI ÚLTIMA OBRA ES UNA REPRODUCCIÓN DE "LA GIOCONDA"...
21.765
¿DESEA VERLA?
¡POR SUPUESTO! SOY GRAN ADMIRADOR SUYO.
¡HE AQUÍ MI OBRA!
¡PERO QUÉ CUADRO TAN FABULOSO!
MAESTRO, QUIERO HACERLE UNA PREGUNTA.
LA QUE GUSTE, MI AMIGO.
¿CÓMO ES QUE LE HA QUEDADO CON ESA INMENSA SONRISA?
¡AH, ESO...!
PRIMERO LA PINTÉ TAL COMO LO HICIERA EL MAESTRO LEONARDO.
¿Y LUEGO?
¡LE HICE COSQUILLAS CON EL PINCEL!
¡PLOP!

La Gioconda

la Gioconda: the Mona Lisa.

obra: work.

He aquí: here we have. This is a fixed expression. It is not the "yo" form of haber, but rather an impersonal verb.

cosquillas: tickles.

el pincel: the brush.

Subjunctive

#4 La que guste: whichever you like. Indefinite subjunctive.

#6 tal como lo hiciera Leonardo: just as Leonardo did it. Imperfect subjunctive here indicates indefiniteness. It is possible to say "Tal como lo hizo Leonardo." That means exactly as he did it. The way it appears in the comic is more indefinite, less precise, less boastful, and is a more elegant way of speaking.

¡ah, gato!
¡OH, EL QUEQUE QUE LE HICE A CONDORITO!
¡AHI VIENE, JUSTO AHORA QUE LO NECESITO!
YA NO SOPORTO MÁS LAS RABIAS QUE ME HACE PASAR "LUCIFER". QUIERO QUE TE LO LLEVES LEJOS, DONDE YO NO LO VEA MÁS.
¡CÁLMESE, MI REINA, YO ME LLEVO A ESE GATO ANTIPÁTICO!
¡GRACIAS, MI REY!
CHAO, YAYITA, ME LO LLEVO.
LO MÁS LEJOS POSIBLE.
TEMPRANO, AL OTRO DÍA...
SOY UN MUCHACHO AÚN.
HORAS DESPUÉS...
YA PERDÍ LA CUENTA DE LOS KILÓMETROS QUE HE ANDADO. AQUÍ DEJARÉ AL GATO.
LUEGO...
¿QUÉ LE PASÓ, COMPADRE?... ESA CARA.
NO ME DIGA NADA, CUMPA.
QUERÍA DESHACERME DE "LUCIFER", EL GATO DE YAYITA. CAMINÉ COMO CINCUENTA KILÓMETROS POR EL CAMPO. ¡YA NO PUEDO MÁS!
PERO VEO QUE EL GATO AÚN ESTÁ CON USTED. ¿QUÉ PASÓ, COMPADRE?
QUE SI NO LO HUBIESE SEGUIDO NO HABRÍA ENCONTRADO JAMÁS EL CAMINO DE VUELTA, CUMPA.
¡PLOP!

Ah, gato

soportar: to put up with.

Chao: goodbye. This is actually the Italian word "ciao", used often in Spanish. In Latin American countries it is only used for goodbye, and never for hello, as is the case in Italian.

deshacerme de: to get rid of.

vuelta: return.

Subjunctive

#3 Quiero que te lo lleves: I want you take him away. Subjunctive of emotion/ volition.

#3 donde yo no lo vea más: where I won't see him anymore. Indefiniteness. "Donde" --meaning an indefinite place--will take subjunctive.
I want to live in a place where there is no snow = Quiero vivir en un lugar donde no nieve .
However, *My grandmother lives in a place where there is no snow = Mi abuela vive en un lugar donde no hay nieve.*

#11 si no lo hubiese seguido no habría encontrado el camino: if I hadn't followed him I wouldn't have found the road. The word "si" triggers past subjunctive in these "contrary to fact" situations.
If I had read the book, I would have passed the exam =Si hubiera leído el libro, habría aprobado el examen.
If she hadn't found the score she wouldn't have learned the song =
Si no hubiera encontrado la partitura no habría aprendido la canción.

LA CITA
1.525-
¡ADELANTE!
¡BUENOS DÍAS! ¿EL SEÑOR CONDORITO?
¡EL MISMO! ¿EN QUÉ PUEDO SERVIRLO?...
YO SOY EL NUEVO COBRADOR DE PÉREZ Y PÉREZ LIMITADA.
¡AHÁ!
¿Y QUÉ PASÓ CON EL SEÑOR GONZÁLEZ? ERA TAN SIMPÁTICO. YA ME HABÍA ACOSTUMBRADO A ÉL.
LO DESPIDIERON, PORQUE NO LOGRÓ NUNCA QUE USTED LE PAGARA... ESPERO QUE CONMIGO NO PASE LO MISMO.
LA CUENTA ES TAN ANTIGUA, QUE YO CONSIDERO QUE ES UNA VERGÜENZA Y UNA MOLESTIA PARA USTED QUE LE VENGAN A COBRAR CASI TODOS LOS DÍAS. ¿NO CREE?
¡HUM!
TIENE TODA LA RAZÓN. ¿QUÉ DÍA ES MÁS CÓMODO PARA USTED?
VEO QUE NOS ENTENDEMOS... ¿QUÉ LE PARECE EL SÁBADO?
DE ACUERDO... ¡PERFECTO!
¡VENGA ENTONCES TODOS LOS SÁBADOS!
¡PLOP!

La cita

cobrador: bill collector.

lo despidieron: they fired him.

no logró: he didn't succeed.

vergüenza: shame.

Subjunctive

#5 no logró que Ud. le pagara: he didn't succeed (in making) you pay. This a past subjunctive of the emotion/ volition type. "Lograr" will, of course, also trigger subjunctive in the present.

#5 Espero que conmigo no pase lo mismo: I hope the same thing doesn't happen to me. Present subjunctive of emotion/ volition.

#6 (es) una molestia para Ud. que le vengan a cobrar: It's a bother for you that they come to collect. Present subjunctive of emotion/ volition. Es una molestia; es terrible; es extraño; es imposible-- all these impersonal expressions take subjunctive.
It's a bother that we have to write compositions so often = Es una molestia que tengamos que escribir composiciones con tanta frecuencia.

VIEJA
¡MIRA, CONDORITO, ES DOÑA PETROLINA!
ASÍ ES, HUEVODURO.
YO CREÍA QUE YA SE HABÍA MUERTO DE VIEJA.
NO, HUEVO.
¡SI HUBIERA MUERTO DE VIEJA, ESTARÍA MUERTA HACE YA MUCHO TIEMPO!
¡PLOP!

CASTIGO

YA ESTÁ AHÍ ESE PAJARRACO HABLADOR.
¡BUENOS DÍAS, DON CUASIMODO!
CONDORITO, ¿OÍSTE ANOCHE CUANDO MI MUJER CASTIGABA AL PERRO?
¡SÍ, LA OÍ...
... INCLUSO OÍ CUANDO LE QUITÓ LAS LLAVES PARA QUE NO SALIERA EN EL AUTO!

ALEGRE
¿CUÁNDO CAMBIARÁ ESA CARA DE VINAGRE?
ESCÚCHEME BIEN, PAJARRACO...
...YO NO SOY NINGUNA AMARGADA, SOY LA PRIMERA EN REÍRME DE MIS TONTERÍAS.
¡CARAMBA! ¡NO SABÍA QUE LLEVABA UNA VIDA TAN ALEGRE!
¡PLOP!

Vieja

Subjunctive

#3 si hubiera muerto de vieja, estaría muerta: if she had died of old age she would (already) be dead.
Here is past subjunctive used with contrary-to-fact "if".
If I had read the book, I wouldn't have seen the movie = Si hubiera leído el libro, no habría visto la película.

Castigo

castigaba: was punishing

Subjunctive

#3 le quitó las llaves para que no saliera: she took the keys so that he wouldn't leave.
Past subjunctive with "para que".
I returned the book, so that my father wouldn't have to do it = Devolví el libro para que mi padre no tuviera que hacerlo.

Alegre

amargada: embittered person.

tonterías: foolishness.

llevar una vida: to lead a life.

#3 No sabía que llevaba una vida tan alegre: I didn't know you lead such a happy life. No subjunctive here, although it could take it. The subjunctive would lend more of a subjective coloring to the sentence. "No sabía" often triggers a past subjunctive of negation. *I didn't know he spoke French = No sabía que hablara francés.*

Quiz VIII: Past Subjunctive

1. I wanted to buy a dog that didn't bark.

2. What did you want me to do?

3. What a shame that he didn't study more.

4. I didn't believe she had the book.

5. It didn't seem that he spoke French.

6. It was impossible for her to have read the book.

7. There was no-one to explain it to me.

8. The dog wanted the girl to feed him.

9. She hoped he hadn't forgotten the i.d.

10. I gave Mary the book before she left.

11. We feared that he hadn't bought the ticket.

12. He didn't have a document that identified him.

13. The doctor prohibited me from smoking.

14. They got him to return their papers early.

15. That girl talked to me as if I were a fool.

16. The children went out without their mother seeing them.

17. It would have bothered her boyfriend having Claudia dance with someone else.

18. My parents didn't want me to miss the movie.

19. The company was looking for an individual who would know something about computer science.

20. She felt sorry that her friend had had a lot of trouble with his girlfriend.

21. Was there anybody there that had been to Argentina?

Section IX

Review

COMERCIANTE
¿ASÍ QUE ESTÁ DEDICADO A LOS NEGOCIOS, COMPADRE?
SÍ CUMPA. DESCUBRÍ QUE MI VERDADERA VOCACIÓN ES EL COMERCIO...
ESTOY DEDICADO A LA DISTRIBU-CIÓN DE PRODUCTOS AVÍCOLAS Y CEREALES FAENADOS...
¡QUÉ BIEN, COMPADRE! LO FELICITO SINCERAMENTE...
GRACIAS, CUMPA. COMPRENDO QUE SE SIENTA ORGU-LLOSO DE TENER UN COMPADRE COMO YO...
BUENO..., LO DEJO, CUMPA. EN ESTE PRECISO MOMENTO TENGO QUE ATENDER MIS COMPROMISOS COMERCIALES...
VOY Y VUELVO... ¡PERMISO!
AL RATO...
CONDORITO
TIMBRE
¡¡¡TORTILLAS DE RESCOLDO Y HUEVOS DUROOOS!!!
¡PLOP!

Comerciante

productos avícolas: poultry products

cereales faenados: refined cereal products.

compromisos: engagements.

tortillas de rescoldo: hot tortillas.

Subjunctive

#3 comprendo que se sienta orgulloso: I understand that you feel proud. This is subjunctive of the emotion/ volition category.
I understand that you are having difficulty with the subjunctive = Entiendo que tengas dificultades con el subjuntivo. This type of use implies compassion. However, *I understand that Evanston, Il., still observes a dry law = Entiendo que en Evanston, Il. todavía se observa la ley seca.* Why no subjunctive? Because this sentence is an impersonal observation, with no empathy or feeling to it.

PROTESTA
CONDORITO, VAYA A LA SALA DE COMPUTACIÓN Y TRÁIGAME LOS DATOS FINANCIEROS DE LA EMPRESA.
¡BIEN, SEÑOR!
6867
RATO DESPUÉS...
¡CARAMBA QUE SE DEMORA ESTE HOMBRE! IRÉ A VER QUE LE PASA...
PERO... ¿QUÉ SIGNIFICA ESTO?
¡HACE RATO QUE LE PEDÍ QUE ME LLEVARA LOS DATOS Y USTED AQUÍ HACIENDO AGUJERITOS AL PAPEL!
¡ES POR CULPA DE LA COMPUTADORA, SEÑOR!
¿QUÉ PASA CON LA COMPUTADORA?
¡LE PEDÍ LOS DATOS QUE USTED DESEA, PERO ME LOS DIO EQUIVOCADOS!
¿Y ESO QUÉ TIENE QUE VER CON QUE USTED ESTÉ JUGANDO CON ESTOS PAPELES?
¿CÓMO QUE JUGANDO? ¿QUE NO VE QUE LE ESTOY ESCRIBIENDO UNA CARTA DE RECLAMO?
¡PLOP!

Protesta

los datos: the data.

la empresa: the firm.

caramba: gosh.

equivocado: mistaken.

reclamo: complaint.

Subjunctive

#4 le pedí que me llevara los datos: I asked you to bring me the data. Past subjunctive of the emotion/ volition class.

#7 qué tiene que ver con que Ud. esté jugando?: what does that have to do with you playing? The subjunctive is triggered by indefiniteness. The speaker is doubtful about the relation between the mistaken information and Condorito punching holes in paper.

Suppose a student says he wants to postpone next Wednesday's test. His reason is that two weeks ago his dog died. The teacher's reaction might be *What does your dog's death have to do with you missing the next exam?* This sentence would be *¿Qué tiene que ver la muerte de su perro con que Ud. falte al examen?*

¡QUÉ ALEGRÍA, PLOMAZO! ¡TE TENDRÉ CORTITO!
NO CREO QUE TENGAS SUERTE.
¿DE QUÉ HABLAS?
MÍRAME BIEN.
21.833
¡LOS IDIOTAS SERÁN ENROLADOS TAMBIÉN!
HABLO DE MI VISTA.
ESO NO ES PROBLEMA. ¡TE RECLUTAREMOS IGUAL!
¡NO PUEDE SER POSIBLE!
¿QUIERES APOSTAR, LINGOTE?
¡NO!.. ¡NO PUEDES HACERME ESO!
¡YO NO QUIERO IR AL FRENTE!
¡POR MÁS QUE PATALEES, NO HAY ARREGLO!
¿NO TE DAS CUENTA QUE SOY CORTO DE VISTA?
ESO TIENE SOLUCIÓN
¡TE METEREMOS EN LA TRINCHERA MÁS PRÓXIMA AL ENEMIGO, JETÓN!
¡PLOP!
¡PLOP!

Corto

plomazo: conveys the idea of heavy or boring.

reclutar: to recruit.

apostar: to bet.

patalear: to kick.

trinchera: trench.

jetón: fathead (loosely translated).

Subjunctive

#1 no creo que tengas suerte: I don't think you'll be lucky (in this). This is subjunctive of doubt and disbelief.
She doesn't believe that I know Madonna = Ella no cree que yo conozca a Madonna.

#6 Por más que patalees: no matter how much you kick. This is subjunctive of the indefinite class. How much can he or will he kick?
If, however, you look at "por más que" as something you have done--that has been accomplished--it will then take indicative.
Por más que estudio no entiendo la geometría. This means the person has indeed studied geometry, but with no success. In this episode, however, no kicking has been done yet.

TODO, TODO, TODO...
¡ES DE ESPERAR QUE ESTE APROVECHADO ME PAGUE LO QUE ME ADEUDA!
23.524
¡CONDORITO...! ¡CONDORITO!
¡PÁSELE, DON MÁXIMO, LA PUERTA ESTÁ ENTREABIERTA!
¡VENGO A QUE ME PAGUES LO QUE ME DEBES, CONDORITO!
¿SABE, DON MÁXIMO? YO LE VOY A PAGAR TODO, TODO, TODO.
SÍ, PERO ¿CUÁNDO?
¡EN CUANTO ESCRIBA MI MEJOR NOVELA!
¡BIEN, CONDORITO...! ¡PERO EN CUANTO YO VEA QUE UN LIBRO TUYO SALE A LA VENTA, VENDRÉ A QUE ME PAGUES TODO!
¡DE ACUERDO, DON MÁXIMO...! LE DOY MI PALABRA DE HONOR.
TIEMPO DESPUÉS...
¡CARAMBA...! ¡IRÉ DE INMEDIATO A COBRARLE AL PAJARRACO!
EL HOCICÓN
GRAN ÉXITO HA TENIDO EL ÚLTIMO LIBRO DEL FAMOSO ESCRITOR CONDORITO.
CONDORITO, AHORA QUE HAS ESCRITO ESE SENSACIONAL LIBRO, VENGO PARA QUE ME PAGUES LO QUE ME DEBES.
OIGA, DON MÁXIMO...
...¿Y QUIÉN LE HA DICHO A USTED QUE YO NO SOY CAPAZ DE ESCRIBIR ALGO MEJOR?
¡PLOP!

Todo, todo, todo

fresco: fresh guy, wiseguy.

en cuanto: as soon as.

a la venta: on sale.

gran éxito: big success.

Subjunctive

#1 es de esperar que me pague : it's to be hoped for that he pays me. Emotion/ volition.

#3 Vengo a que me pagues: I'm coming so that you pay me. "A que" functions like "para que", and triggers subjunctive.

#4 en cuanto escriba: as soon as I write. "En cuanto" and "con tal de que" both mean "as soon as" and both trigger subjunctive.

#5 en cuanto yo vea: as soon as I see. See previous note.

#7 vengo para que me pagues: Similar to #3 above. This time the trigger is "para que".

HISTORIAS
¡CÓMO NOS VAN A ENVIDIAR EN PELOTILLEHUE CUANDO SEPAN QUE EN ESTA CONVENCIÓN DE ALCALDES NOS HAN ALOJADO EN EL PISO 80 DE ESTE EDIFICIO.
¡SEÑORES, LAMENTO INFORMARLES QUE EL ASCENSOR ESTÁ FUERA DE SERVICIO!
BIEN. ¡SUBIREMOS POR LA ESCALA!
¡OCHENTA PISOS!
8.034
PROPONGO QUE CADA UNO CUENTE UNA HISTORIA QUE DURE 20 PISOS, ASÍ LA SUBIDA NO SERÁ TAN PESADA!
¡ESTÁ BIEN! EMPEZARÉ.
PISO 20...
...Y DEL TIPO NUNCA MÁS SE SUPO.
¡JA, JA, JA!
¡JA, JA!
PISO 40...
...¡Y EL ÚNICO QUE CAZÓ UN PATO FUE EL CURITA!
¡JA, JA! ¡AHORA ME TOCA A MÍ!
PISO 60...
¡CREO... QUE... MI HISTORIA... NO LES VA A GUSTAR!...
¿POR QUÉ NO NOS VA A GUSTAR, PAJARRACO AGUAFIESTAS?
¡UUF!
¡PORQUE... LA LLAVE... SE NOS QUEDÓ... EN... LA RECEPCIÓN!
¡PLOP!
¡PLOP!

Historias

alojar: to house, to lodge.

fuera de servicio: out of order.

piso: floor.

un pato: a duck.

el curita: the priest.

pajarraco: stupid bird.

Subjunctive

#1 cuando sepan : when they find out. This is a future-directed "cuando", and so requires the subjunctive.

#4 Propongo que cada uno cuente: I propose that each one tell. Emotion / volition, caused by the verb "propose". Other similar triggers are "insistir", "recomendar" and "aconsejar".

#4 una historia que dure 20 pisos: a story that lasts 20 stories. Indefinite quantity: any tale that will last 20 stories.
I need a pen that writes in 3 colors =Necesito una pluma que escriba en tres colores.

ADVERTENCIA
¡AY! ¡QUÉ TARDE ES! OJALÁ YAYITA ESTÉ LISTA.
¡OH, MI AMOR! ¡AL FIN LLEGASTE!
SÍ, YAYITA. TEMÍA QUE AÚN NO ESTUVIERAS ARREGLADA.
ESPÉRAME, AMORCITO. ME VOY A DESPEDIR DE MAMÁ.
NO TE DEMORES, YAYITA.
ME VOY, MAMÁ.
SI VAS A SALIR CON ESE PAJARRACO, QUIERO QUE REGRESES TEMPRANO.
PERO, MAMÁ... SI YA NO SOY UNA NIÑA.
¡POR ESO MISMO QUIERO QUE VUELVAS TEMPRANO!
¡PLOP!

Advertencia

no te demores: don't delay.

por eso mismo: for that very reason.

Subjunctive

#1 Ojalá Yayita este lista: I hope Yayita is ready. Emotion/ volition subjunctive in the present tense.

#2 Temía que aún no estuvieras arreglada: I feared you weren't ready yet. Emotion/ volition subjunctive in the past tense.

#4 quiero que regreses temprano: I want you to return early. Emotion/ volition.

#6 Quiero que vuelvas : I want you to return. Emotion/ volition.

A BUEN ENTENDEDOR...
ES DEMASIADO TARDE PARA QUE YUYITO ESTÉ TODAVÍA VIENDO TELE CON CONÉ, YAYITA.
YO PENSÉ QUE CONÉ SE HABÍA IDO, MAMÁ. CONDORITO DEBE ESTAR MUY PREOCUPADO.
¡OYE, CONÉ, YA ES HORA DE QUE YUYITO SE ACUESTE!
¡BIEN!
¡ELLA NO PODRÁ SEGUIR VIENDO TELE!...
¡BIEN!
...ESTEE... COMO NOS IREMOS TODOS DEL LIVING, APAGARÉ EL TELEVISOR...
¡BIEN!
CLIC
CONÉ, ENTIENDE. YA ES HORA DE QUE TE VAYAS A CASA.
¡BIEN!
TREMENDO DISCURSO QUE SE MANDÓ PARA DECIRME QUE ME FUERA.

A buen entendedor

viendo tele: watching T.V.

apagar: to turn off.

discurso: speech.

Subjunctive

#1 Es demasiado tarde para que Yuyito <u>esté</u> viendo tele: It's too late for Yuyito to be watching T.V. The subjunctive is caused by "para que": a special type that we've seen. This type acts like a comparison between her (a little girl) and someone else watching late t.v.

#4 Es hora de que Yuyito se <u>acueste</u>: It's time for Yuyito to go to bed. This is emotion / volition, and always causes subjunctive. (a fair translation of this trigger would be " it's <u>about</u> time that...)

#7 Ya es hora de que te <u>vayas</u> : it's time for you to go. See previous note.

#8 Tremendo discurso quese mandó para que me <u>fuera</u> : What a big speech that was raised to tell me to leave. Emotion/ volition in the past, triggered by "mandar".

OBSESIÓN
BIEN, SEÑOR ZALDÍVAR, LO ESPERO A COMER ESTA NOCHE EN MI CASA.
GRACIAS, ALLÍ HABLAREMOS.
TODO MI FUTURO DEPENDE DE QUE ESTE CABALLERO ME FIRME ESE CONTRATO. FUE BUENA IDEA INVITARLO A COMER.
CREO QUE PUEDO DAR POR HECHO EL NEGOCIO.
¡HOLA, TÍO!
¡CONÉ! NO HABÍA PENSADO EN ESTO... DEBERÉ ADVERTIRLE.
MIRA, TÍO, TODO ESTÁ LISTO PARA RECIBIR A ESE CABALLERO TAN IMPORTANTE.
TÚ SABES LO IMPORTANTE QUE ES PARA MÍ QUE EL SEÑOR ME FIRME ESE CONTRATO.
POR ESO DEBO ADVERTIRTE QUE EL TIENE UN DEFECTO. POSEE UNA ENORME NARIZ.
¡JA! ¡JA!
CUALQUIER BROMA QUE LE HAGAS A ESE CABALLERO Y PERDERÉ EL CONTRATO. SI ESO OCURRE, TE DARÉ UNA PALIZA.
SÍ, TÍO.
ESTOY NERVIOSO: PRONTO LLEGARÁ...
...Y CONÉ NO PODRÁ AGUANTAR LA RISA AL VER SU GIGANTESCA NARIZ, Y...
¡ADIÓS, NEGOCIO!
CONTINÚA...

¡JA! ¡JA! ¡JA!
¡BUENAS NOCHES, CONDORITO! ¡Y SOBRE ESE CONTRATO, ES MEJOR QUE LO OLVIDE!
QUÉ INGENUO SOY. PENSÉ QUE INVITARLO A COMER ERA UNA BUENA IDEA.
Y AL FIN LLEGÓ EL SEÑOR ZALDÍVAR...
LA COMIDA ESTUVO EXQUISITA. GRACIAS POR INVITARME.
CONÉ NO DICHO NINGUNA BARBARIDAD. NO DEBO CONFIARME.
OJALÁ NO LO HAGA CUANDO YO VAYA A LA COCINA A SERVIR EL CAFÉ. NO QUIERO NI PENSARLO.
TÍO...
¡REFLAUTA! LLEGÓ EL MOMENTO FATAL.
TENGO MUCHO SUEÑO. ME VOY A LA CAMA. BUENAS NOCHES, SEÑOR.
¡INCREÍBLE!
¡QUÉ NIÑO TAN EDUCADITO! BUENAS NOCHES, HIJO.
¡QUÉ ALIVIO! AHORA PUEDO ESTAR TRANQUILO.
Y PENSAR QUE NO PUDE COMER NADA ESPERANDO QUE CONÉ DIJERA UN DISPARATE SOBRE LA RIDÍCULA NARIZ DEL SEÑOR ZALDÍVAR.
CAFÉ
ESTEEE... SEÑOR ZALDÍVAR, ¿CUÁNTAS NARICES DE AZÚCAR LE PONGO EN EL CAFÉ?
¡PLOP!

Obsesión

dar por hecho: take for granted.

advertirle: caution him.

una paliza: a beating.

aguantar: to hold in.

ingenuo: naive.

barbaridad: outlandish remark (here).

disparate: crazy remark.

Subjunctive

#2 mi futuro depende de que me firme: mi future depends on him signing. The trigger here is "depender" which implies possiblity and uncertainty.

#6 lo importante para mí que el señor firme: How important for me it is that he sign. The trigger is "es importante".

#8 cualquier broma que le hagas: any joke that you do. "Cualquier broma" implies indefiniteness. "Whatever joke you pull."

#12 es mejor que lo olvide: it's best that you forget it. Emotion/ volition, triggered by "es mejor".

#15 Ojalá no lo haga: I hope he doesn't do it. Emotion/ volition.

#15 cuando yo vaya : when I go. This is a future-directed "cuando", and requires subjunctive.

#19 No pude comer nada esperando que Coné dijera... : I couldn't eat anything waiting for Coné to say... Emotion/ volition in the past subjunctive. The trigger is "esperar".

Quiz I: Emotion /Volition

Suggested translations

1. Me encanta que entiendas de mecánica.

2. Ellos quieren que les compremos el cuaderno.

3. Es mejor que vayan al aeropuerto temprano.

4. El jefe no permite que fumemos en la oficina.

5. Les exijo que pongan más atención en los detalles.

6. El dentista me dice que haga una cita para el mes que viene.

7. Si Ud. demora mucho, arriesga a que el libro no esté en el estante.

8. Es una gran cosa que tú hables tantos idiomas.

9. Propongo que nos reunamos otra vez la semana que viene.

10. Es de esperar que no olvide la tarea.

11. Te pido que me ayudes con el proyecto.

12. No quiero que lleguen temprano.

13. Me encanta que vengas a mi casa tan seguido.

14. Le molesta al profesor que yo conteste en inglés durante la clase.

15. Mamá siempre nos pide que hagamos la cama.

Quiz II : Para que

1. Es muy temprano para que vayamos a la fiesta.

2. Trabajo mucho para que me aprecie el jefe.

3. Dejaron una lista en la mesa para que haga las compras.

4. Para que haya paz en el mundo necesitamos más comprensión.

5. Para que no se confundan pueden encontrar las respuestas en las últimas páginas del libro.

6. Voy a ayudar a mi hermano para que pueda salir temprano.

7. Ella va a entregar la composición hoy para que la profesora se la devuelva más pronto.

8. La gata maulla mucho para que su dueña se despierte en la mañana.

Quiz III: Dudar/ Parecer/ Creer

1. No me parece que tenga suficiente plata para comprar el coche.

2. No creo que la conozcan.

3. ¿Crees que Phil Collins tenga mucho pelo?

4. Ella no cree que entienda el libro.

5. Creen que John conduce bien.

6. Dudan que pueda jugar el juego.

7. Parece que están en la oficina hoy.

8. Duda que podamos hablar bien el español en menos de un año.

9. ¿Crees que vayan a México el próximo mes?

Quiz IV: Time

I. Cuando me gradúe quiero encontrar trabajo en México.

2. Me quedo en casa hasta que me llame Jane.

3. Tenemos que terminar la composición antes que el profe regrese.

4. Cuando trabajo mucho me canso.

5. Cada vez que llegues tarde, recibirás una multa.

6. Empezaremos el proyecto después de que llegue John.

7. Tan pronto como terminemos tenemos que irnos.

8. Los niños pelean hasta que alguien se hace daño.

9. Los estudiantes no se pueden ir para la casa hasta que les diga el profesor.

10. Cuando vengas a Chicago, por favor no te olvides de visitarme.

11. Tan pronto como lo sepa, te haré saber.

Quiz V: Negation

1. No hay día en que el profesor no llegue temprano.

2. No hay nada en libro que clarifique el concepto.

3. No tiene nada de malo que pidamos prestado la chaqueta.

4. No es que el libro sea difícil sino que e s muy largo.

5. No veo a nadie que tenga el libro.

6. No hay nadie que sepa donde está la llave.

Quiz VI: Indefinite

1. ¿Hay un libro aquí que explique el subjuntivo?
2. Busco un gato que tenga un temperamento agradable.
3. Tal vez pueda sugerirnos algo que nos ayude.
4. ¿Tiene un documento que lo identifique?
5. Quiero comprar un perro que no ladre.
6. Necesito un lapicero que escriba en tres colores.
7. El que termine primero recogerá los exámenes.
8. El que hable otro idioma, que se levante.
9. Busca una corbata que le haga juego al saco.

Quiz VII: Present perfect

1. Espero que haya comprado el pan.
2. No parece que hayan estudiado mucho.
3. No creen que hayamos visto la película.
4. Es imposible que Juan haya terminado el libro tan rapidamente.
5. Es de esperar que todavía no han enviado la carta.
6. Es extraño que no hayas tratado de terminar la composición.
7. Probablemente no hayan devuelto los libros todavía.
8. Es una tontería que no haya comprado su boleto todavía.
9. Siente mucho que Uds. hayan llegado tarde.
10. ¿Hay alguien en la sala que no le haya entendido al profesor?
11. Temo que el perro haya comido el pastel.

Quiz VIII: Past Subjunctive

1. Quería comprar un perro que no ladrara.

2. ¿Qué querías que hiciera?

3. Qué lástima que no estudiara más.

4. No creí que tuviera el libro.

5. No parecía que hablara francés.

6. Fue imposible que hubiera leído el libro.

7. No había quien me lo explicara.

8. El perro quería que la nina lo alimentara.

9. Esperaba que no hubiera olvidado el carnet.

10. Le di el libro a María antes de que se fuera.

11. Temimos que no hubiera comprado el boleto.

12. No tenía ningún documento que lo identificara.

13. El médico me prohibió que fumara.

14. Lograron que les devolviera las composiciones temprano.

15. Esa chica me habló/ hablaba como si yo fuera tonto.

16. Los niños salieron sin que la madre los viera.

17. Le habría molestado a su novio que Claudia bailara con otro chico.

18. Mis padres no querían que yo me perdiera la película.

19. La compañía buscaba a un individuo que supiera algo de informática.

20. Le daba lástima que su amigo hubiera tenido tantos problemas con su novia.

21. ¿Había alguien allí que hubiera estado en Argentina?

APPENDIX: USES OF THE SUBJUNCTIVE

Most Spanish grammar textbooks present an overall view of the subjunctive as being divided into different types of clauses that are formed by two phrases. These phrases are linked, for the most part, by the word "que". Some students find this terminology confusing. This book doesn't employ these terms, but rather has grouped subjunctive into easy-to-understand categories: emotion/ volition, negation, para que, etc. However, in the interest of completeness, here is a brief exposition of the subjunctive types in traditional grammar terminology.

1. Noun clauses

Usually, in a noun clause the subjunctive relates to a developed relationship between the speaker and what the speaker specifically desires, intends, wishes, either from or for someone else. It is at this point that students should familiarize themselves with many different verbs that trigger the subjunctive.

Luis quiere que María venga a la fiesta
(Luis wants something from María-- that she come to the party)
El padre deseaba que le fuera muy bien a su hija.
(Her father wished her to be succesful)

2. Adjective clauses

Here students have to become familiarized with the term "antecedent" given that the subjunctive refers back to it.

Aquella compañía desea contratar a una persona que sepa por lo menos una lengua extranjera.
(The antecedent is a hypothetical foreign language speaker)
Aquel chico encontrará a alguien que le hable en español.
(The antecedent is hypothetical: someone who will speak Spanish)

3. Adverbial clauses

Students have to become familiar with expressions such as "para que", "a menos que", "sin que" etc., Conjunctions of time, such as "cuando", "tan pronto como", etc. may also require the subjunctive if the action of the main verb hasn't yet occurred.

Queremos aprender mucho para que el profesor se sienta orgulloso.
Juan se fue de la sala de clase sin que el profesor lo viera.

4. If clauses

"If" clauses trigger the imperfect subjunctive (never the present subjunctive) if and when the "if" clause is a highly hypothetical statement, followed by the conditional or the past conditional; a contrary -to-fact statement is stated with the pluperfect subjunctive, followed by the past conditional.

Si trabajaras más, tendrías más dinero para el mes.
Si hubiera ido al cine, habría visto a mis amigos.

"Como si" and "ni que" require the imperfect or the pluperfect subjunctive.

Me hablas como si fuera un niño.
Ni que se hubiera casado con la reina de Inglaterra.

All Condorito comics reproduced with the kind permission of World Editors, Inc., Santiago, Chile. Special thanks go to their General Director, Sergio Pumarino V.